The
INTERNATIONAL
RELATIONS
of
THE BIBLE

Other Books by Lamont Colucci

Space, Grand Strategy, and United States National Security,
Praeger International Security, 2022

The National Security Doctrines of the American Presidency:
How They Shape Our Present and Future,
a two-volume set in the Praeger Security International series, 2012

Crusading Realism:
The Bush Doctrine and American Core Values After 9/11,
Lanham, Maryland, Rowman & Littlefield, 2008

Coauthored Books

Homeland Security and Intelligence,
ed. Keith Gregory Logan, Praeger, 2017

The Impact of 9/11 on the Media, Arts, and Entertainment:
The Day That Changed Everything?,
ed. Matthew J. Morgan, Praeger, 2009

The
INTERNATIONAL
RELATIONS
of
THE BIBLE

Lamont Colucci

Post Hill
PRESS

A POST HILL PRESS BOOK

The International Relations of the Bible
© 2021 by Lamont Colucci
All Rights Reserved

ISBN: 978-1-64293-227-0
ISBN (eBook): 978-1-64293-228-7

Interior design and composition by Greg Johnson, Textbook Perfect

Luttwak, Edward N. *The Grand Strategy of the Roman Empire: From the First Century CE to the Third.* Fig 1.2, p. 22–23; Map 1.2, p. 30–31; Map 2.1, p. 64–65; Map 2.2, p. 92–93; Map 2.7, p. 120; Map 2.8, p. 123. © 1976, 1979, 2016 Johns Hopkins University Press. Reprinted with permission of Johns Hopkins University Press.

Post Hill Press
New York • Nashville
posthillpress.com

Published in the United States of America
1 2 3 4 5 6 7 8 9 10

To my wife, Kathryn,
and our children
Isabella, Alfred, and Roland.

Contents

Preface

This book has been in the making for two decades. It started as a "nice project" that I could do someday, overtaken by numerous publications I undertook on hard power national security and grand strategy. However, always in the back of my mind, I returned to this topic. Because more of my writing on national security and grand strategy was foundationally dependent on biblical principles, it made less and less sense for me to not write the book that should have come before all the others.

I expect a multitude of criticism from various corners, and my first recommendation for those individuals is to read the first page of Chapter 1 very carefully. This book has particular parameters and does not masquerade as anything else.

Further, I presume there will be heavy criticism from the atheist and agonistic community that cannot, and will not, accept the Bible as the literal Word of God and therefore will dismiss the contents herein. I can only invite those people to embrace God's word and see no value in participating in antagonism. I would say the same to the religious believer who is not Jewish or Christian.

Finally, the camp that I refer to as "Christian lite" will play at being both religious and skeptical. I can only refer them to what C. S. Lewis most famously said, often referred to as the Lewis trilemma:

> I am trying here to prevent anyone saying the really foolish thing that people often say about Him: I'm ready to accept Jesus as a great moral teacher, but I don't accept his claim to be God. That is the one thing we must not say. A man who was merely a man and said the sort of things Jesus said would not be a great moral teacher. He would either be a lunatic—on the level with the man who says he is a poached egg—or else he would be the Devil of Hell. You must make your choice. Either this man was, and is, the Son of God, or else a madman or something worse. You can shut him up for a fool, you can spit at him and kill him as a demon or you can fall at his feet and call him Lord and God, but let us not come with any patronizing nonsense about his being a great human teacher. He has not left that open to us. He did not intend to.

The Christian only has one choice open to him regarding the Bible. It is either the Word of God, or it is not. If it is not, then one has to reconsider one's labels.

Finally, the years of research and thinking about this has produced many conclusions. You will read many of them in this book. Our understanding of the ancient world and antiquity is built on mountains and mountains of evidential shreds, minimal primary sources, and speculation and theories built on more preexisting pinnacles of speculation and opinions. If anyone claims they know the truth about the biblical period that is outside of the Bible, they are being less than truthful. As a scholar-practitioner in the field of international relations and national security, I bring to the table just that perspective; you are getting the analysis of a person from that vantage point who is also a Christian. We embrace experts because we have confidence they use their education, skills, intelligence, and wisdom to create ideas and theories. However, more importantly—much more—experts should reach conclusions and solutions, or else their value is dubious. Academics and armchair philosophers who "just like to ask questions" or, worse, question the absolute nature of truth, should reflect on the plummeting value of academics in the public square.

CHAPTER 1

International Relations and the Bible

For the kingdom is the Lord's:
and he is the governor among the nations.

—PSALMS 22:28

The subject of international relations and the Bible may appear to some as a strange one. The Bible is not a treatise on foreign affairs, nor are most international relations academics concerned with the Bible. Yet it seems equally odd that the most important book ever written, ever published, and ever sold has never been looked at through an international relations lens. This book will combine eras and themes of the world of international relations as the backdrop to the Bible.

Now that we know what the book is about, we need to discuss what the book is not. This book is neither a history of the Bible nor a classicist analysis of the period or of translations. There are plenty of works that do those things.

Further, this book is not out to prove the historicity of the Bible. It is also not a religious or theological text. It is neither more or less than what it purports to be. All biblical references will be from the King James Version and are accepted as the literal Word of God. The book agrees with the tenets described by Pastor James Montgomery Boice:

God created the world; God is in control; God is revealed through the Bible; people have rebelled against God and can be redeemed, though not all desire redemption; all history and creation exist for the glory of God. Thus, the supremacy of the Bible as God's word is recognized.

The book will describe the world of the Bible in terms of international relations, not take history or international relations and explain them in terms of the Bible. The secular progressive academic community is full of sophomoric questions such as whether or not the kings of Israel, like David and Solomon, existed, or worse, question the existence of Jesus. As many readers know, there is plenty of historical and archaeological evidence that is considered extra-biblical. This evidence ranges from the thirteenth century BC stele celebrating the Egyptian pharaoh Merneptah's military victories known as the Merneptah Stele, mentioning Israel to Jewish sources like Flavius Josephus and the Talmud to Roman sources such as Cornelius Tacitus, Gaius Suetonius, and Pliny the Younger. All of these sources mention many biblical figures, such as Herod the Great, Herod Antipas, Pontius Pilate, John the Baptist, James (the brother of Jesus), Antonius Felix, Porcius Festus, Publius Sulpicius Quirinius, and of course, Jesus.

This book will illustrate the points of convergence between the biblical, the natural, and the supernatural.

A right way of thinking about this historical period is to divide it, the way many in the clergy have done, into three parts: sacred history, which is the history *in* the Bible; a secular history, which is not directly mentioned in the Bible; and redemptive history, which is specifically related to Jesus and salvation. Equally childish to questioning the existence of Solomon and Jesus is the current fad to use the dating system BCE and ACE rather than BC and AD. My most challenged students quickly see through the veil of wokeness, noting that the so-called common era is derived from the birth and resurrection of Jesus.

The center of international relations for the majority of discovered civilized history in the Western world has been located in and around the Mediterranean Sea and the Fertile Crescent. From the third century

BC onward, the primary narrative has been driven by the classic movements in international relations: control, ideology, military power, economic resources, and trade.

In 1973, James Fees of the CIA talked to Secretary of State Henry Kissinger. Fees informed Kissinger that a memo existed detailing the turmoil in the Middle East, including the problems in the Sinai and Iranian expansion into places like Yemen. Kissinger was shocked, since he assumed someone was leaking classified information, until Fees informed him that the memo was written in 700 BC. We are reminded of the book of Ecclesiastes 1:9:

> The thing that hath been, it is that which shall be; that which is done is that which shall be done: and there is no new thing under the sun.

The Bible is the most popular book in human history. It has been translated, studied, fought over, and loved by countless millions. It is, therefore, astounding how little most Jews and Christians know about the historical time period that the Bible describes. More importantly, it is the lack of knowledge about international relations that serves as the omnipresent backdrop of every significant biblical event.

The singular subject of international relations is both a scholarly field for academics and students as well as a practical arena for everyone else, not just politicians and diplomats. It regulates everyone's life beyond calculation. It determines job prospects, economic growth and decline, war, peace, and whether or not a foreign entity uses a weapon of mass destruction. The practice and theory of international relations, diplomacy, war, and economics is grounded in theories and ideologies used by leaders around the world since the beginning of civilization.

Terms

You can get lost in the jargon of international relations. Luckily, you don't have to remember too many terms in order to understand the basics. Diplomats often talk "interests": vital, national, and peripheral. Vital interests are existential. They mean survival. For example, the United States had a vital interest in what the Soviet Union did with its nuclear weapons. National interests are the critical interests for your nation's military position, economic prosperity, and stability. For example, Japan has a national interest in the free flow of oil through the Persian Gulf. Peripheral interests are those that you like or want but are not critical. For example, the United Kingdom has a peripheral interest in human rights in its former colonies.

Politicians and academics use terms like "state" or "nation" sometimes as if they are the same. The state is the government, the border, the capital city, the legal code, and the currency. The nation is the people, the culture, the values, and the shared history or language. States can be nations, nations can be states, but they can also be separate. The United States is a state and a nation. Afghanistan is a state (barely) but not a nation. The Kurds are a nation but not a state. In biblical times, we are lower down this hierarchy of state and nation when we talk of kingdoms and higher up when we speak of empires. The reader should remember that an empire is not always a power with an emperor. Republican Rome and democratic Athens were both militaristic and expansionistic empires, as were the Israelites under King David.

Finally, you might see terms like "unitary state," which simply means a single power with a single government, such as modern-day Israel. The opposite of this is a "transnational organization," which is a group that exists across many borders, like the terrorist group ISIS. This book will also deal with terms like "terrorists," "pirates," and "assassination." The latter two terms are obvious, but there is a debate historically and today about the term "terrorism." Those that believe in absolute moral values, such as Christians and Jews, realize there is an abstract definition of terrorism whose variables include motivation (political/religious), victims (the innocent), and methods (violent). Those that reject absolute moral values often use the quote attributed to the terrorist leader of the Palestine Liberation Organization: one man's freedom fighter is another man's terrorist. Take the case of George Washington to debunk Arafat. He did not order attacks against civilians during the Revolutionary War, and so he would not be a terrorist under the first definition but would be if you used the second definition.

International Relations Theory

Primarily, international relations, or IR theory, has focused on states and states at war. IR theory tries to make sense of conflict in places like Syria, Israel, and Afghanistan. IR theories primarily reflect the nation-state to nation-state conflicts of the early and mid-nineteenth and twentieth centuries. Traditional IR theory struggles to account for transnational terrorist groups like al-Qaeda. This is because those terrorist groups did not play as an essential factor in the nineteenth and twentieth centuries as they do in the world we live in today. (The Black Hand may have lit the match in World War I, but it was not the root cause.) International relations theory for the United States has been a triangular battle between realism, liberalism, and a third alternative, sometimes referred to as democratic realism, which I call crusading realism. Added to this mix are grand strategy theories of strategic disengagement, balance of power, offshore balancing, and primacy.

Grand strategy is the long-term strategy (possibly over centuries) a nation implements by harnessing military, economic, and political power to advance its position. This is especially important when looking at the empires depicted in the Bible. Although there are new age IR theories with labels like positivist, constructivism, Marxist, feminist, or post-positivist reflectivist based on issues of class and gender, these seem to be purely abstract exercises at best. They offer nothing to how statecraft is engaged. They further tend to reject God and the Bible out of hand. Needless to say, the Marxist and social constructivist interpretations of IR, based on economic materialism, imperialism, gender, and dependency, might make for interesting thought experiments in the back rooms of dark think tanks, but little else. However, they fail to answer any questions about how international relations actually work.

This failure is even more significant when applying those theories to analyze the eras of the Bible. IR theory is grounded in a belief in attitudes concerning human nature. It is natural for Christians to think about, since Christianity acknowledges a sinful, fallen humanity. Marxists, for example, are devoted to the exact opposite belief: the perfectibility of man and the creation of an earth-bound utopia. This is the second most important question that any theory of politics must grapple with. The first question revolves around one's belief in the truth. The crux of Christianity and Judaism believes in eternal, immutable, God-given truths. Other theories preach a version of relativism with values changing over time, distance, location, people, and culture.

Realism

Realists focus first on the question of human nature. Historical realists, including those writing at the time of the Bible, and classical realists of the nineteenth and twentieth centuries, have focused on the innate nature of human beings needing to dominate others, believing that this is amplified by the actions of states. It is often characterized as a pessimistic or evil view of humankind. This IR debate can be summed up by the notion that there is one world of realism and responsibility and another of idealism and good intentions. Today, neo-realists are more apt to explain the dog-eat-dog world of realism as a systemic problem based on world anarchy. However, all realists focus on the need to control rapacious men, whose human nature cannot be changed by force. War is bound to occur. Every nation, kingdom, and empire pursues its own interests. Since the world has no single leader or government, there is anarchy, which creates the eternal condition for violence and conflict. This is an unending struggle.

A policy based on force is neither moral nor immoral. Realists focus on the unitary (single) state, on interests and not ideology, on peace through strength, and on the balance of power. They are wary of universalistic notions of morality. Further, they assert that Western societies often operate on a dual moral standard: one standard for the citizens in their own country (moral liberalism) and another for nondemocratic foreign countries (realism). In this same vein, historical realists have stressed that different times in history create different moral levels of behavior for state survival. Realists believe that states are always seeking power over other states and, if possible, tried to position themselves into maximum power. Some conservative scholars would argue that international relations are even more straightforward than realism, that it is merely the study of power, world order, and empire. Henry Morgenthau's famous line, "International politics, like all politics, is a struggle for power," is as complex in its ramifications as it is simple in appearance.

Married to realism, crusading realism contains many of the assumptions to which realists in international affairs subscribe. The state is still the supreme actor, canonized in the Peace of Westphalia in 1648. The primary actors are geographically-based (the United States and the state sponsors/abettors of terrorism), and the anarchy of the world system creates inherent aggression among states to seek power. It is different than realism because it promotes the idea that statecraft must be the servant of morality. The noble goals of democracy, human rights, and the rule of law must be the ultimate goal, not merely the achievement of power. This should strike a particular chord with Christians and Jews.

The United States, as the world's global order maker, is a good and continuous reference point. If the crusading realists were only concerned with stability and balance of power strategies, the emphasis would not be on promoting democracy in such places as Iraq, Lebanon, Uzbekistan, and Ukraine. Realism, by itself, fails to address the crusading aspect, arguably the most powerful element of the foreign policy shift of the last two decades. Furthermore, realism assumes rational actors on the world's stage. Although it is not the purpose of this book to argue the rationality of the Kim dynasty of North Korea or of al-Qaeda, Islamo-Bolshevism, or terrorist leaders like Osama bin Laden, questions about their rationality arise in a way that did not concerning the leaders in the Kremlin during the Cold War. Lastly, many realists will agree with the crusading realists about current US primacy, but they see the use of unparalleled power very differently. Michael Mandelbaum argues that the United States is perceived as the Philistine Goliath but is actually an *ordungsmacht*, or order maker, like the sun in the center of the solar system:

> The sun keeps the planets in their orbits by the force of gravity and radiates the heat and light that make life possible…similarly the United States furnishes services to countries, the same services, as it happens, that governments provide within sovereign states, to the people they govern. The United States, therefore, functions as a world government.

Primacy is the desire of both crusading realists and realists to ensure that the United States is the supreme power in international affairs. The point of divergence between the two is of particular concern to Christians and Jews—what to do with that power? Is it for power's sake to prevent a rival as the realists want? Or is it to make the world better and assist others toward a path of democracy, human rights, and the rule of law as the crusading realists believe? However, as successful as realism has been, and it certainly is the dominant force behind the empires in the Bible, it is equally unsatisfying to the Jew or Christian concerned about justice and morality. In fact, the realism used by the imperial powers in the Bible demonstrates the stark contrast between God and man, and in particular, the life and legacy of Jesus Christ.

Liberalism

Classical liberal internationalists, along with their more modern counterparts, have focused on the positive aspects of human nature and the excellent benefit mankind can obtain from international organizations. They believe in the Enlightenment concepts of human perfectibility, rationalism, faith in progress, and harmony of interests. Whether this is based on right reason or because of enlightened self-interest is an internal liberal debate. A recent development is the growth of the democratic peace theory. It suggests that democracies don't war against each other (though they may have quite vicious wars with nondemocratic states). Crusading realists would be very comfortable with the democratic peace thesis, except that it only focuses on diplomacy and economic leverage as opposed to force. Crusading realists are willing to use force in the service of virtue, even if the use of that force is unpopular.

Some argue that liberalism is the fundamental characteristic of American foreign policy filtering all policy options. In other words, liberalism advocates argue that America's liberalism makes some policy options impossible, and it controls the American level of commitment. Thus, if Americans are crusaders, they are reluctant crusaders, driven by pragmatism, fenced in by liberal values. In order to understand this, you can think of the debates about assassination, covert operations, or the treatment of battlefield detainees in places like Guantanamo. You can be assured that the ancient biblical empires and the modern Russian and Chinese states feel no trepidation in using any action the way modern America does. America holds itself to an unparalleled moral standard, a biblical standard.

Liberalism in international relations definitely promotes the Wilsonian ideal of self-determination and democracy. It rests on the premises of multilateral cooperation, successful international organizations, and the combining of power with the desire for economic (usually capitalist) prosperity. It received a positive injection because of the horrors of World War I. That war was seen as so catastrophic that many thought any option was better than war.

In many ways, this was the Clinton administration's assumption about the international world. Thus, classical liberalism may offer idealism, but it is idealism without force. For example, liberalism failed to stop Hitler in 1938 when Western leaders chose appeasement under cover of liberal diplomacy. In other words, liberal values are high sounding and pseudo-moral, but they lack authority since liberals are so fearful to use force, especially maximum force. They fear being accused of disproportionality or striking first.

Crusading Realism

Since 9/11, a very American IR theory took hold during the Bush administration. Its roots are inherently biblical. However, crusading realism cannot exist without the victory of Enlightenment-thinking married to Christian values. Thus, the pre-democratic, historical, moral alternative to classical liberalism and crusading realism is simply moral realism. Moral realism was and is a mixture of a moral compass and realistic goals in international affairs. This is illustrated in biblical terms with the Kingdom of Israel, which was mostly obedient to God under such leaders as David, Solomon, Hezekiah, and Josiah, and then under the Greco-Romans when they mixed ideas about universal law with their statecraft.

The concept of democratic realism or crusading realism refers to an approach centered on four basic principles: preemption, prevention, primacy, and democracy promotion. Thus, crusading realism combines realism and liberalism that shows America as it really is. In essence, it is the culmination of over two hundred years of policy and history rather than the neo-left-wing theories so popular today. In reality, the tensions created by crusading realism stretch back into American foreign policy history, which some authors have illustrated as a battle between righteous realists (like President Theodore Roosevelt) and self-righteous idealists (like President Woodrow Wilson). It can easily be argued that the doctrine is simply the culmination of the forces that created the American state. It is this elementary idea that is lost on many academics and policymakers whose inability to grasp this has led to such polarization of the debate. In other words, there is now a widespread inability to understand the role of, what was called in the 1950s, the democratic morality in American foreign policy. Needless to say, this point alone does not neutralize criticism of this very American approach. George Kennan, the famous diplomat and realist practitioner, wrote in 1951 an early warning to such crusading when he said:

> But where your objectives are moral and ideological ones and run to changing attitudes and traditions of an entire people or personality of a regime, then victory is probably something not to be achieved entirely by military means or indeed in a short space of time at all.

In essence, this judgment sums up many of the modern realists' grave concerns about the shift in American foreign policy away from what they would term the solid foundation that policies like containment were based upon. Many realists continue to see crusading realism as an extension of realism, or even realism on steroids. Primacy is a common theme for crusading realists, although there is debate among many scholars as to whether it is imperial primacy (for empire) or hegemonic primacy (for world order).

Most importantly, realists have failed to take into account the most revolutionary aspect of crusading realism—democracy promotion. It is crucial to our discussion; crusading realists base their arguments on antiquity, with the supremacy of the Bible at its core. The fundamental center of their universe is the survival of Western civilization and that America represents the joining and culmination of Jerusalem, Athens, Rome, and London.

Finally, in contrast to the above is a small school, sometimes referred to as Christian realism, founded by the liberal theologian Reinhold Niebuhr. It embraced the tenets of Christianity, especially those referred to as the Great Commandment or the first two of the Ten Commandments. It rejects natural law and just war theory that was outlined by the Roman Catholic Church and many conservative Protestants. It assumes that humankind's sinfulness combined with free will always produces evils such as genocide, and therefore compromises in international relations have to be made. It misunderstands the depth of the eternal conflict in American foreign policy between morality and realism, which has been a constant tension created by American commitments to biblical teaching.

The Bible, America, and International Relations Theory

American concepts of IR theory and practice stemmed from a fundamental belief in natural law. Initially presented by Greco-Roman philosophers as a universal law, it became the fundamental approach by Christian theologians of the Middle Ages, such as St. Thomas Aquinas. It progressed under Enlightenment political philosophers such as John Locke for natural law to be God's law, emanating from the Bible. It is the American belief in the inherent dignity of the human spirit, where all humankind is allowed the freedom to practice their God-given liberties of life, liberty, and estate (and happiness as the happiness to pursue virtue). God wanted mankind to be free from the fear created by the tyranny of distant kings of the past, or of extremist groups like al-Qaeda, or from rogue regimes like Iran now.

Thus, there can be no American Revolution without the Declaration of Independence, which based its entire legitimacy on natural law, bestowed by God himself. It was the one bright line that separated the American Revolution from every other revolution. However, there can be no natural law without the Bible.

The American Founding Fathers invoked the grand natural laws, expressed best by John Locke, linking the natural divine laws of life and liberty to those of property and territorial claim.

The rising star of American independence rested on the foundation that liberty under law was the natural extension of the Creator's wishes, and that those who oppose liberty oppose the natural order itself. This is the view that America represents a universal nation and is the actual manifestation of natural law and natural rights of liberty under the law.

In simple terms, the single most important event in the history of international relations, the American Revolution, was legitimate and successful only because it rested on the foundation of the most important book to humanity, the Bible. There would be no Western concepts of human rights, universal justice, just war, or the Geneva Conventions without the biblical impact on international affairs.

The Biblical Era and International Relations

International relations dominate the Bible. This is the situation during the Egyptian, Babylonian, Persian, and Parthian empires; the influence of Greek Hellenism; and the critical role played by the Romans. It is an omnipresent backdrop.

It would be impossible and fruitless to write a date-by-date history of international relations in the Bible. There is also the problem that the Old Testament covers four thousand years of history as compared to the New Testament, which includes about one hundred years. This book will primarily focus on the period from the kingdoms of Israel to the destruction of the Second Temple in 70 AD.

This book is also divided into eras and themes. The chapters are based on the periods in the Old and New Testament. This is the biblical world in all its mystery and brutality. It was a world very different from the modern one, where standards of life, death, politics, and morality are foreign, removed by place and time. It was a world, like our own, of great power, where conflict between powerful nations shaped the political, military, and economic world around them. During the biblical period, the great powers were Egypt, Parthia, and Rome. Today, the United States holds the preeminent position, followed by nations like China, Russia, India, and the United Kingdom, yet still impacted by smaller nations like Syria, Israel, Lebanon, Iran, and North Korea.

War is a central theme of the Bible, especially waged by and against the people of Israel. In many ways, it holds one of the center stages in biblical conflict and change. Terrorism, though not a term until the

French Revolution, is part and parcel of the world of the Bible, with groups like the Zealots and sicarii engaging in brutal and often important actions.

The goal of peace, whether by treaties between kingdoms like Israel and Persia, or the peace of Christ, is illustrative of humankind's attempt to avoid conflict. Diplomacy, by the great powers, is another river that flows through the Bible, sometimes in good faith, sometimes with treachery. The various kingdoms and empires of the Bible engage in foreign policy throughout the Old and New Testament. Economic globalization, products, and merchants are illustrated in the Bible with stories ranging from trade and commerce between Egypt and Canaan to the Three Wise Men. Human rights, slavery, and freedom are the final themes, illustrated by the various enslavements of the people of Israel, the constant of the slave trade in the entire ancient world, and the liberation and freedom given by Jesus.

The international relations context changes one's reading of the Bible. It does not challenge God's word; it only explains the human motivations that enable the reader to understand the gaps in the Bible. These are not religious or theological gaps. The Bible is not a history text or political treatise. However, by understanding specific international relations themes, one can understand the background of biblical events.

Examples are many: Joseph is enslaved in Egypt because his brothers are jealous of his God-given favor. The Hebrews are forced by economic conditions to seek trade with the one power that has the resources they need. This supernatural and natural reason combine to create Joseph's situation. The rulers of Lower Egypt at the time were the Hyksos, who like many barbarian-style takeovers in history (like the Mongols in China) had become absorbed into the more sophisticated Egyptian culture. It was, therefore, most likely a Hyksos pharaoh who promoted Joseph and encouraged Jewish emigration. Once the indigenous Egyptians were back in power, they were likely to have enslaved the Jews due to their needs as a kingdom. Here, we can reflect and argue that there can be no story of Exodus without the impact of international relations, first by trade in the case of Joseph's brothers and then by power needs as in the case of the enslavement of the Jews.

It was international relations that explain the human motivations behind the Babylonian captivity. Judah's (Israel's) attempted and failed diplomacy to play Egypt off of Babylon would ultimately lead to the Hebrews being on the wrong end of that great power conflict; thus, it was their mistake, combined with King Nebuchadnezzar's expansionist policies. In the supernatural realm, they fell from God's favor. Their mistakes in the natural world of foreign affairs led them to the second great enslavement of the Jewish people and the story of Daniel. International affairs would again intervene to change the situation once the Persians defeated the Babylonians and the Jews were allowed to return. This clearly illustrates themes of human rights, slavery, diplomacy, and great power conflict.

This region has always been the international relations mix of turbulence and movement. We can see parallels in today's Israel, Lebanon, and Syria, which have always been a crossroads for trade, commerce, war, and the clash of civilizations, due to its geopolitical location.

International relations would intervene again with the conquests of Alexander the Great, which would Hellenize the entire geographic area depicted in the Bible. This would create the conditions for the growth of Gentile communities, which would be of pivotal importance to Roman rule, but more importantly, to the evangelizing of Christianity by St. Paul to Gentiles, ultimately leading to its supremacy to all of Western civilization.

However, no international relations effect was greater than that of Rome. The entire New Testament and the deeds of Jesus are entirely interwoven against a Roman backdrop. Why was Rome in the region? How did it rule? How can we understand Rome's attitudes? Rome collected taxes via the *publicani* (publicans) system so critical to many biblical accounts. The apostles and their enemies traveled on Roman roads and were confronted with either the lawlessness or lawfulness of Roman rule.

We consider the impact Rome had on our biblical events, and it is shocking. The subjugation of the Greeks, Egyptians, and the rest of the Mediterranean led to the conquest of Judea under the expansive Roman Republic. The Jews lost their independence due to Rome's titanic conflict in the Third Mithridatic War (in modern-day Turkey) to ensure Rome's overseas empire was protected. This led to the installation of the Herodian dynasty under Herod the Great. Judea would eventually be placed under the Roman province of Syria at the beginning of the New Testament under the legate Quirinius and subject to the hated census of Augustus (leading to Joseph and Mary's trip to the stable in Bethlehem). Later, Judea was under the local command of the prefect Pontius Pilate. The role of St. Paul and the crucifixion of Jesus all took place under Roman administration.

This period of Roman rule clarifies the background of New Testament Judea. It also explains the relations between the Jewish and Gentile communities and even why the infamous Judas Iscariot was a member of an anti-Roman terrorist organization known as the sicarii. Indeed, Rome's impact extends well beyond the crucifixion. In mundane ways, this was shown when the early Church co-opted Roman titles and administration units for creating Christian institutions, and in major ways through evangelizing to the Gentiles until Rome and even its emperors and legions fell under Christianity's sway.

Human rights and just war utilized the Roman foreign policy of *fides* (good faith) and *pietas* (piety), later incorporated into Christianity. However, the most significant impact on international relations was from Jesus. Jesus completely transformed our concepts of justice, human rights, just war, justice in war, honesty in trade, and liberation.

We would not even have debates about theories or ideologies of international relations in the Western world without Jesus's teachings. There would be no alternatives to realism, no limitations on war, no fearful command to be honest in trade, no civilized treatment of prisoners of war, and no demand for human dignity without His legacy.

CHAPTER 2

The Old Testament
and International Relations

Let every soul be subject unto the higher powers.
For there is no power but of God: t
he powers that be are ordained of God.

—ROMANS 13:1

The Old Testament covers a historical period of around 1,200 years and is dominated by the story of the Jewish people. These are the first five books of the Bible, called the Pentateuch: Genesis, Exodus, Leviticus, Numbers, and Deuteronomy. These are the books of law. This is followed by the books that are categorized as history, poetry, and prophetic words: Joshua, Judges, 1 and 2 Samuel, 1 and 2 Kings, 1 and 2 Chronicles, Ezra, Nehemiah, Esther, Job, Psalms, Proverbs, Ecclesiastes, Song of Solomon, Isaiah, Jeremiah, Lamentations, Ezekiel, Daniel, Hosea, Joel, Amos, Obadiah, Jonah, Micah, Nahum, Habakkuk, Zephaniah, Haggai, Zechariah, and Malachi.

Unique among ancient people was Jewish belief in monotheism and their battle not only with polytheistic foreign enemies but amongst their own constant descents into paganism. What was also unique was that the state and the religion were a synthesis; one could not exist without the other, producing a version of theocracy and what in modern international relations refers to as a nation that predates the current state of Israel.

The ancient Jews subscribed to three pillars: one God, one Torah, and one Temple. These formed the foundations of the nation. These pillars begin to be illustrated by Noah, circa 2515 BC, and the giving of the Noahide Laws, which are alluded to in the Bible and depicted in the Talmud. The implications for IR are that these laws of God are universal and serve as one of the cornerstones of what would become the Western concept of human rights and even international law—laws that today govern nations that wish to be right-acting.

Since this is not a history of the ancient world, a brief discussion of the empires that serve as a backdrop to the Bible will be brief. The ancient world was warlike and dangerous, with the survival of any kingdom based on military strength. During the biblical period, Jerusalem alone was sacked and/or razed to the ground on at least twenty occasions. The bulk of the Old Testament is dominated by the Egyptians, Hittites, Assyrians, Babylonians, and Persians. The intertestamental period was dominated by the Greek and Macedonian empires, followed by the empire of the Roman Republic, which, around the time of the New Testament, transitions to the imperial Roman Empire. Before Abraham, Pharaoh Amenemhet I stated, "None hungered in my years or thirsted in them, men dwelled in peace through that which I wrought." Later, King Hammurabi (mentioned in the Bible as Amraphel in Genesis 14:1) echoed this with, "Bring the four quarters of the world to obedience." These empires contended with each other in a realist game of power, diplomacy, war, and competition for resources.

Egypt

The Egyptian Empire was dominated by the rule of the pharaohs, who were considered to be half man and half god. It was, therefore, a theocratic-style authoritarian dictatorship. The first pharaoh was Narmer (Menes), ruling around 3100 BC. Egypt is mentioned abundantly in the

Figure 2-1: Ancient Egyptian Empire

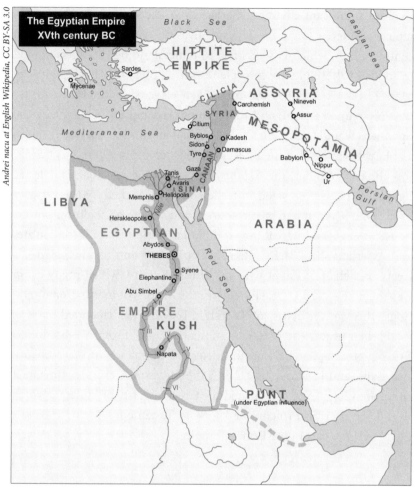

Figure 2-2: Egyptian Empire, 1500 BC

Bible—it appears in Genesis, Exodus, Leviticus, Numbers, Deuteronomy, Joshua, Judges, Samuel, Kings, Chronicles, Nehemiah, Psalms, Isaiah, Jeremiah, Ezekiel, Daniel, Hosea, Amos, Micha, Nahum, Haggai, Zechariah, Matthew, Acts, Hebrews, Jude, and Revelation. At its height, around the fifteenth century BC, it dominated the modern countries of Egypt, Libya, Sudan, Israel, Lebanon, and Syria.

The significant dividing marker of Ancient Egyptian history is often considered to be the Hyksos invasion (eighteenth to sixteenth centuries BC), which is so critical to understanding the international relations of the Bible. Joseph (Genesis 37:4, 39:2–12, 41:1–12, 45:1–28; Mark 15:42–47; Acts 7:9) was most likely elevated by the Hyksos ruler possibly named Apopi, and the eventual reconquest of Egypt by the Egyptians would lead them to conquer Canaan and create buffer states.

Egypt is integral to the Bible, including its role in Abraham's travels, Joseph's enslavement, the Exodus, and providing sanctuary for Jesus. Egypt was heavily engaged in trade and lived or died by the vagaries of the Nile River. It had vast resources and was an agricultural power-house. It engaged in great power diplomacy and war with the Hittites and Assyrians. In 1274 BC, Ramses II (Genesis and Exodus) signed a treaty on behalf of Egypt with the Hittite Empire, which many claim was the first recorded peace treaty in the history of international relations. This was the Treaty of Kadesh in 1269 BC, which ended the war, established peace, and created a mutual alliance. From 728 BC to 332 BC, Egypt experienced war and defeat at the hands of the Nubians, Assyrians, and Persians. In 332 BC, the forces of Alexander the Great conquered Egypt and established the Greek dynasty of Ptolemy, which would play a critical role in the later Old Testament. Finally, in 31 BC, Egypt became part of the Roman Empire.

Hittites

The Hittites (descendants of Ham) began their expansion into central Turkey around 2000 BC, and through periods of victory and defeat, expanded under a series of kings who were both the secular ruler and the high priest to a malleable polytheistic religion, notable for storm gods. It appears that the government was a monarchy that contended with an assembly (Pankus) of nobles. Their economy was primarily based on agriculture, livestock, and mining. They were known to have been exceptional ironworkers of the Iron Age.

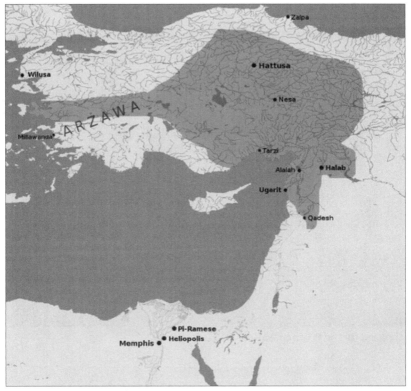

Figure 2-3: The Hittite Empire

The Hittites appear in the Old Testament in Genesis, Exodus, Numbers, Deuteronomy, Joshua, Judges, Kings, Chronicles, Ezra, and Nehemiah. They sold Abraham a burial ground; Rebekah was noted to have despised them; Esau and Solomon marry Hittite women; and of course, Uriah, whom King David killed, was one.

The Hittite Empire reached its zenith in the thirteenth century BC, where it dominated modern-day Turkey and northern Syria. It contended against the Jewish people and the empires of Egypt and Assyria. In 1245 BC, the Hittites were defeated by the Assyrians. Before being absorbed into the Assyrian Empire, they were defeated by the Phrygians. Most scholars contend that Assyria obliterated the remnants of the Hittites.

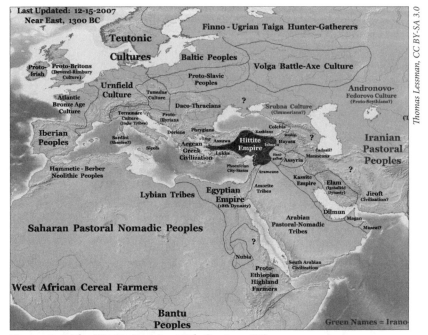

Figure 2-4: The Hittite Empire, 13th Century BC

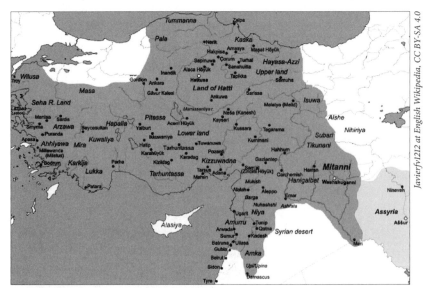

Figure 2-5: Assyrians Defeat Hittites

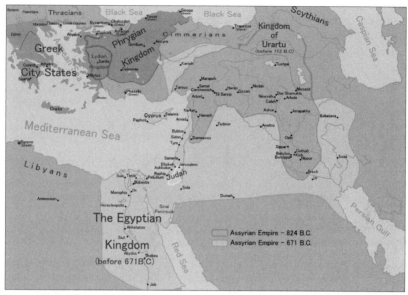

Figure 2-6: Map of Assyria

Assyrian Empire

The Assyrian Empire was actually a series of empires from 2000 BC onward. Assyria appears in Kings, Isaiah, Lamentations, Ezekiel, Hosea, and Micah; and its capital, Nineveh, is mentioned in Genesis, Kings, Isaiah, Johan, Nathan, Zephaniah, and Matthew. It contended with all of its neighbors for power and dominated the region from 1363 BC to 600 BC, reaching its zenith under the New Assyrian Empire from 1000 to 600 BC, encompassing modern-day Iraq, southern Turkey, Syria, Lebanon, Israel, Jordan, and Egypt. It was a monarchy divided up into provinces ruled by governors. Its economy was driven by agriculture, livestock, and control over trade routes. They were a pagan people famous for their ziggurat temples.

In the Old Testament, Assyria is portrayed as a cruel and despotic power that sought the destruction of the Jewish people. Assyria destroyed the northern Kingdom of Israel and was used by God to

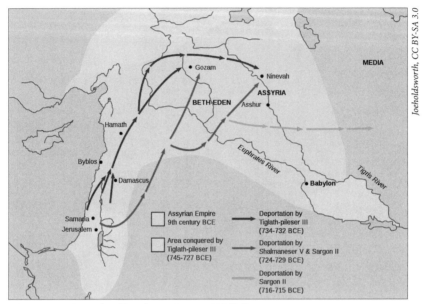

Figure 2-7: Assyrian Empire, 1000 to 600 BC

punish Israel for its paganism in the book of Isaiah, and its capital Nineveh was where Jonah was sent to preach God's judgment. During the reign of Hezekiah, the Kingdom of Judah, up to the gates of Jerusalem, was despoiled until God slew 185,000 Assyrian soldiers.

The Assyrians were infamous for their harsh and exploitative practices, especially in taxation. In 612 BC, the capital city of Nineveh was captured by an alliance between the Babylonians, whose capital was plundered by the Assyrians, and the Medes, who were also bent on revenge.

Babylonians

Like the Assyrians, the Babylonians built a series of empires. The Babylonians are encountered in Genesis, Kings, Psalms, Isaiah, Jeremiah, Daniel, Peter, and Revelation. The first Babylonian Empire was under Hammurabi, who ruled from 1792 BC to 1750 BC and created a

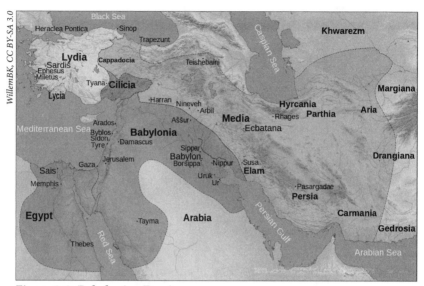

Figure 2-8: Babylonian Empire

kingdom that dominated the Euphrates River valley. This empire was short-lived, and Babylon was sacked by the Hittites in 1595 BC. A new Chaldean dynasty seized control and created a new empire or Neo-Babylonian Empire from 626 to 539 BC, which conquered the Assyrians. At its height, it dominated the modern countries of Iraq, Syria, Jordan, Lebanon, Israel, and parts of Saudi Arabia and Egypt. The government was similar to Assyria, a monarchy with provincial governors. They were also pagans with their chief god depicted as a dragon, Marduk. Their economy, especially under the Neo-Babylonian period, was vast and abundant in resources of agriculture, livestock, weapons, precious metals, jewelry, and wood. They achieved this by dominating intricate trade routes.

Babylon plays a critical role in the Old Testament. One of its significant figures was Nimrod, who was a descendent of Cush, builder of the Tower of Babel; and in the biblical tradition, he and Babylon become a synonym for all that is in rebellion to God. Babylon is evil.

God punishes the Jewish people for their transgressions by allowing the Babylonians to conquer and subjugate them.

It was Nebuchadnezzar II who captured Jerusalem in 597 BC, forced the elite into exile, and established a puppet ruler. Jerusalem rebelled after a failed diplomatic effort to align with Egypt and was conquered again in 586 BC, which resulted in the infamous Babylonian captivity, the failure of the fiery furnace, and the Temple of Jerusalem to be burned and destroyed. During the captivity, the prophets Ezekiel and Daniel, who were from Judah, appear, and Daniel ascends to be a royal advisor where he foretells the fall of Babylon to Persia. Babylon serves as a marker for evil all the way through to the book of Revelation 18:21:

> And a mighty angel took up a stone like a great millstone, and cast it into the sea, saying, Thus with violence shall that great city Babylon be thrown down, and shall be found no more at all.
>
> In 539 BC, the last Babylonian king went into exile as the Persians conquered them.

Persia

If Egypt, the Hittites, Assyria, and Babylon were touchstones of evil in the Old Testament, Persia serves a different role for the Jews and is found in the books of Chronicles, Ezra, Esther, Ezekiel, and Daniel. In 559 BC, Cyrus II became king of part of Persia and began expanding against the Medes. In 550 BC, the Median army changed sides to Cyrus, and he inherited an empire to become Cyrus the Great of the Achaemenid Empire and began a conquest of the entire region. Babylon succumbed to him due to the people's revulsion of its royal family's incompetence and abandonment of Marduk. The peak of the Persian Empire was in the fifth century BC, when it had conquered modern-day Iran, Iraq, Turkey, Syria, Lebanon, Israel, and parts of Egypt, Libya, Saudi Arabia, the Gulf States, India, Greece, Macedonia, and Bulgaria.

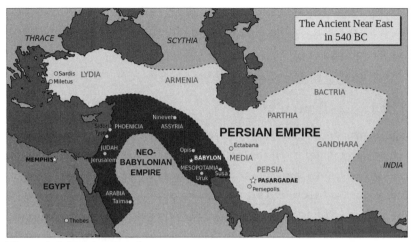

Figure 2-9: Persian Empire

The government was like that of an absolute monarch that ruled through satraps, (similar to provincial governors) and relied on an intricate bureaucracy. The economy was naturally global in its breadth and depth, with great wealth and influence.

The Persians were primarily Zoroastrians, and worship centered on their god, Ahura Mazda, who was in a constant cosmic battle with evil. Scholars debate whether to call this monotheism or dualism, but at least one can argue that it was unlike the religious beliefs of the majority of the earlier empires in the region.

Persia was also pivotal in the Old Testament, beginning with Daniel's prophecies about the fall of Babylon. It would be Cyrus who would free the Jews and restore them their capital and Temple, even providing resources for the rebuilding. Daniel becomes an advisor to Darius, and through God's intervention, he was saved from the lions. Persia is the background to the Feast of Purim, established when Esther saves the Jews from the evil Haman, who was a descendant of Agag the king of the Amalekites, whom Saul did not kill, even though God ordered it. Thus, Persia was used by God to liberate the Jewish people.

The wars with the Greeks from 499 BC to 449 BC would put Persia on the road to destruction, culminating in its conquest by Alexander the Great in 330 BC.

The IR Environment

The international relations environment from an IR theory perspective is rather simple. All the ancient kingdoms operated along classical realist lines until we look at the Kingdom of Israel under Solomon and David, where one can see the underpinnings of moral realism (the ancestor of crusading [democratic] realism). The introduction of Greco-Roman concepts of natural and universal law, *fides*, and *pietas*, especially for the Roman state, also illustrates a battle between Roman realism and Roman moral realism. The birth of classic realism and crusading (democratic) realism only occurs with the legacy of Jesus and the New Testament.

The first international relations atmosphere illustrated clearly in the Bible comes during the time of Abraham, circa 2066 BC, who lived in the Sumerian city of Ur (Genesis 11:28), in what is modern Iraq. Ur was the center of political power in the region and was an advanced civilization with a high standard of living. Yet, Abraham left and traveled by caravan from Ur to Mari, Haran, Damascus, Shechem (Canaan), Egypt, and back to Canaan. Abraham was not called on to create a new religion; he was called to establish a new nation and set into motion one of the most dominant themes in international affairs through today, as this action ushered in the Age of Patriarchs.

Israel—and we will use this term in a generic sense—was ruled by prophets and judges, which was the case until the establishment of a Jewish monarchy. Around 1800 BC, during the Middle Kingdom period in Egypt, there was immigration from Syria and Canaan by people the Egyptians called Asiatics. The Jews that settled in Egypt may have come in large numbers even before this. As mentioned previously, the Hyksos had invaded and conquered part of Egypt and may

Figure 2-10: Journey of Abraham to the Land of Canaan

have elevated these Asiatics to positions of authority and power. This would go a long way to explain the events surrounding Joseph. Joseph could have reached the pinnacle of power when Egypt was ruled by the Hyksos. The Hyksos may have favored the Jews, and just like the canal in Egypt that still bears his name, Joseph was therefore in a position to save Egypt from a famine, assist his family, and have the Jews settle in greater numbers in Goshen.

This would also help explain why, when the Hyksos were pushed out, the "native" Egyptians turned on the Jews. They might have erased much of Jewish history and those who supported the foreign sand-dweller rulers, making Israel a province of Egypt to serve as a buffer between it and the Hittite Empire. Egypt then embarked on the creation of a permanent army and engaged in true empire building, borne in part on the backs of Jewish slaves, leading to the Exodus when Moses received the Ten Commandments. The Ten Commandments were given to Moses on Mount Sinai and serve as the fundamental and universal markers for personal, group, and national moral behavior until

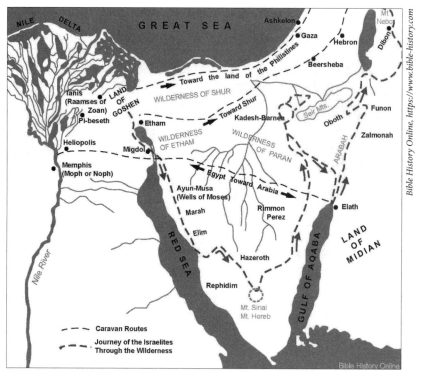

Figure 2-11: Route of the Exodus of the Israelites from Egypt

the teachings of Jesus. The admonishments against murder, thievery, and treachery apply equally to king and commoner, state, kingdom, and nation. The impact of the Ten Commandments on the behavior of nations, international relations, and international law cannot be understated.

Between 1405 and 1390 BC, Joshua led the Jewish people in their conquest of Canaan, creating the actual borders of a Jewish kingdom. This era led to the numerous wars fought for the biblical Jewish homeland. The Jews must obey God (Genesis, Deuteronomy, Samuel, Numbers, Joshua) to execute holy wars and rid the earth of the seven Canaanite nations, which were the Hittites, Girgashites, Amorites,

Canaanites, Perizzites, Hivites, and Jebusites. They were also ordered to crush the Amalekites and Midianites. Saul's failure to properly obey God led, as previously mentioned, to the almost extermination of the Jews during the Persian period by Haman. These actions introduce into the Western tradition of international relations the concept of holy war, which will eventually be termed a crusade during the Christian period.

This era from Joshua onward created the first of two geopolitical phases of biblical Israel. The first from the conquests of Joshua to the Babylonian captivity set the stage for Israel's unique concept of international relations. This was the biblical aspiration of a united, independent nation devoted to God as their primary identity as His chosen people. Israel's geopolitical situation was comprised of a three-way division, starting with a coastal plain stretching from modern Tel Aviv to Haifa, which evolved into a more cosmopolitan, trade-oriented, and worldly culture that exists even today. Second, there was a hilly northern region from Mount Hermon to Jerusalem dominated in part by the harder, more rustic and warlike Galileans. The question of who controlled this area was always a concern, as it was where invaders would be funneled into the Megiddo plain (mentioned in Revelation 16:16 as Armageddon).

Finally, there was an area encompassing Jerusalem to Jordan and the Negev Desert. Two deserts helped to partially protect Israel from hungry neighbors, namely the Negev from Arabia and the Sinai from the Egyptians. The problem area for Israel primarily came from the north, which provided few natural barriers except for the Litani River.

Israel was an international affairs convergence zone for any land empire expanding southward or eastward and any Mediterranean empire that was looking for supplies, ports, and a land bridge into the greater Levant.

One question we need to ask ourselves is why Abraham and his immediate descendants were allowed to establish such a presence in the world of much more powerful neighbors. The answer may lie in Egyptian politics. Canaan is mentioned as abundantly as Egypt in the books

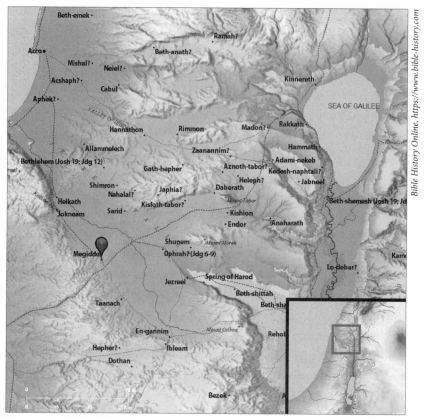

Figure 2-12: Megiddo Plain

of Genesis, Exodus, Leviticus, Numbers, Deuteronomy, Joshua, Judges, Samuel, Kings, Chronicles, Ezra, Nehemiah, Psalms, Isaiah, Ezekiel, Obadiah, Zephaniah, Zechariah, and Matthew. Canaan was originally separate from the great powers of this time. It became a province of Egypt, but during the reign of Pharaoh Amenhotep IV (1353–1336 BC), who became Akhenaten, Egypt was weakened due to his attempts to destroy the polytheistic state religion. It could be postulated that this led to inattention to Canaan, which therefore benefited the Israelites. Thus, the Israelites took advantage of the chaos in Egypt and the divided Canaanites.

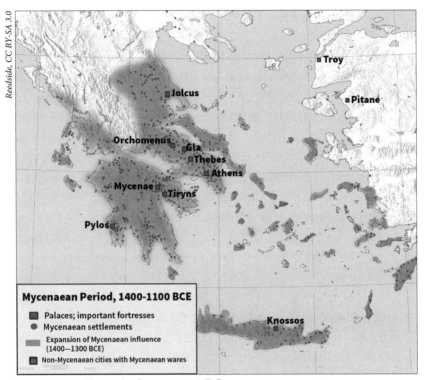

Figure 2-13: Homeric Greece, 1200 BC

The international situation around the time of Homeric Greece (circa 1200 BC) was one where the Hittite kingdom was vanquished by the Assyrians, which had pushed the Sea Peoples, or Philistines, into the land of Canaan. The great power conflict between the Egyptian, Hittite, and Assyrian empires was over trade routes, vassal states, and territory. By the time war broke out between the Philistines and the Jews, there was no central power in the region.

The period in the Bible where a unified Kingdom of Israel exists dates from circa 1020 BC to 930 BC. This encompassed the kingships, appointed by the prophet Samuel, of Saul, David, and Solomon. Secular historians dispute the whole notion of a unified kingdom, although the

Tel Dan stele, which mentions the House of David, may have rebuked some of them.

The Philistines (where we get the word "Palestinian" from) were a warlike and pagan people and are referenced in Genesis, Exodus, Joshua, Judges, Samuel, Kings, Chronicles, Psalms, Isaiah, Jeremiah, Ezekiel, Amos, Obadiah, Zephaniah, and Zechariah. They occupied Canaan, probably from islands in the Aegean like Crete, and posed an existential threat to Israel. In the thirteenth century BC, during the era of Samson and Samuel, the Philistine tyrant kings formed a coalition against the Jews and killed scores of them. Saul was able to hold them at bay but would eventually be killed by them. David beat the Philistines' greatest warrior, Goliath, and Hezekiah finally ended the threat posed by them. They, like the Babylonians, were a reference marker for evil and sinfulness.

It was King David (1004 BC to 965 BC), not Saul, who changed the international relations situation for the region. It was David who brought low the Philistines. David (Samuel, Kings, Psalms, Proverbs, John, and Romans) captured Jerusalem and made it the capital of Israel, the legacy of which continues to this day. The king of Israel during this time was viewed as a viceroy of God. David not only solidified control of Israel, but he created a Jewish empire stretching from the Euphrates River to the Red Sea. He encouraged the mining and use of iron and copper. This was the height of Israel on the ancient international scene and would become the aspirational goal of any Jew who dreamed of empire building and reclaiming a worldly kingdom of glory and prestige.

David's son Solomon (965 BC to 930 BC; Samuel, Kings, and Chronicles) consolidated power and expanded the prestige and economy of Israel through diplomacy, treaties, and trade. Solomon's greatest achievement was the building of the Temple, which became the center of both Israel's faith and conflict for generations.

The period from the death of Solomon to the time of Jesus was one of division, chaos, war, oppression, and defeat for the Israelites. In

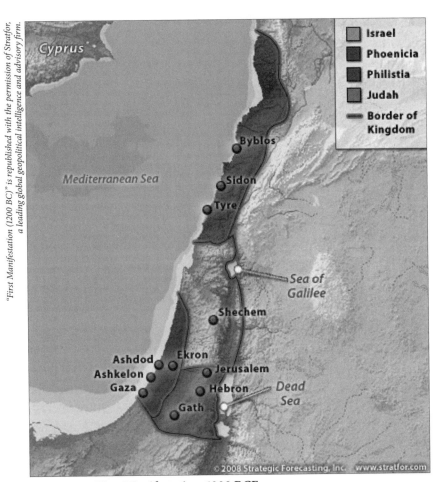

Figure 2-14: First Manifestation, 1200 BCE

the pre-Greco-Roman period, the Jews were divided between a northern kingdom called Israel, with its capital at Samaria, and a southern kingdom, Judah, which still had Jerusalem as its capital. During this period, both kingdoms were pawns of the international affairs situation, subject to wars and conquests by the Egyptians, Assyrians, Babylonians, and Persians and leading eventually to the Israelites' outright conquest and enslavement.

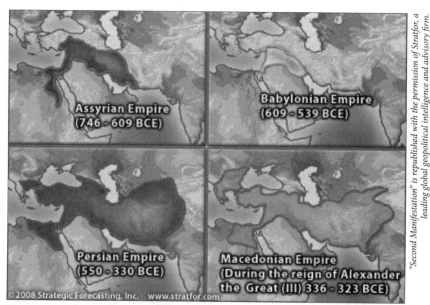

Figure 2-15: Second Manifestation

There were attempts by some Jewish rulers to enter the great game of international politics by trying to play Egypt and Assyria off each other, often becoming vassals of one or the other. This was further exacerbated by the enmity between the northern and southern kingdoms. In 926 BC, the Egyptian pharaoh, at the urging of the king of Israel, Jeroboam (Chronicles), attacked Judah, pillaging the Temple of Jerusalem. The northern kingdom lasted until 722 BC when Assyria wiped it out and carried off its people into slavery. This was most likely done by King Sargon II (Isaiah 20:1), who ruled Assyria from 722 to 705 B.C and forcibly resettled men from Babylon and other regional areas into the former northern kingdom, especially Samaria. This conglomeration of people became the famous Samaritans (Kings, Matthew, Luke, John, Acts) who were from that point onward despised by the Jews as foreign and corrupt occupiers. Later, in an attempt to offer an olive branch, the Samaritans would offer to help rebuild the Temple at Jerusalem but were summarily rebuffed.

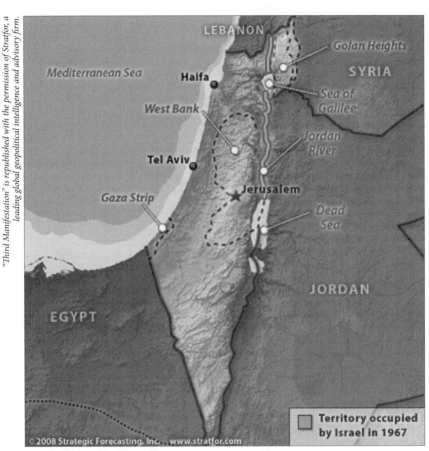

Figure 2-16: Third Manifestation

It must be emphasized how much the Samaritans were loathed and hated by the Jews. There is no group in American history that would be equivalent, not even the Tories after the American Revolution. Perhaps they were seen on the same level as al-Qaeda or ISIS, not as terrorists, but as people to be despised and avoided. This should provide one with incredible context when Jesus interacts with the Samaritans later in the New Testament.

The period where biblical international relations were focused on the Kingdom of Judah showed the second typology of international

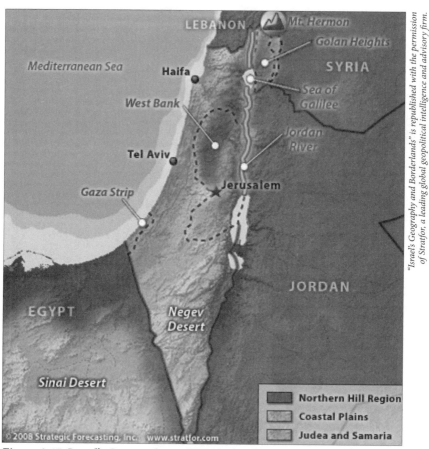

Figure 2-17: Israel's Geography and Borderlands

affairs and the Jews. It was one where there was rebellion against God and miscalculation in foreign affairs, where the people were crushed and the kingdom despoiled.

Judah had more success at staying somewhat free, especially under King Hezekiah (716–687 BC). Hezekiah (2 Kings) consolidated Jewish monotheism and attempted to put the people right with God and his laws. It is important to note that when the kings of Judah were ruled by men who were more in line with God's plan and desires, they tended to prosper and strengthen. On the other hand, when they were ruled by

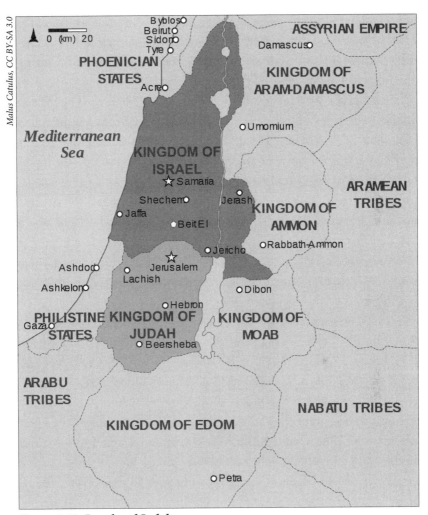

Figure 2-18: Israel and Judah

those who fell away, such as under Ahaz and Manasseh, the state failed. Further, both sets of rulers failed at various attempts to play Assyria and Egypt off one another. Hezekiah attempted the use of balance of power politics to save his kingdom by creating an alliance with Egypt against Assyria. Assyria led by King Sennacherib (2 Kings 18:21) viewed this as an attempt to foment insurgency, and Egypt did not honor its diplomatic commitments, which brought the Assyrian army to the gates of Jerusalem before God's intervention. Although Judah technically became a vassal state of Assyria, Hezekiah had created a strong and powerful nation whose capital he fortified.

Egypt and Assyria's constant fighting was overshadowed by the rise of the Neo-Babylonian Empire. King Josiah (2 Chronicles) of Judah (642–609 BC) enjoyed a period of greater independence due to this fighting. In 609 BC, Josiah took his army to Megiddo to stop the Egyptian army from reinforcing the disintegrating Assyrian Empire against the Babylonians. This power-politics gambit proved fatal, and he died in the battle. The death of Josiah ended the Davidic line and was a crucial turning point in the international relations of the Jewish people as represented by the Judean kingdom. From this point onward, there would be little to represent an independent Jewish kingdom that was not subservient to some other foreign power.

Josiah was replaced by Jehoahaz (609 BC), who ruled for only three months before being kidnapped by the Egyptian ruler Necho II (2 Kings, 2 Chronicles, Jeremiah 46) on his way back to Egypt and replaced with his brother Jehoiakim. This demonstrated arrogance would continue to bedevil Judah when King Jehoiakim (609–598 BC) engaged in bad policy at home and abroad. The Bible informs us that Jehoiakim (2 Kings, 1 and 2 Chronicles, Jeremiah, Daniel) was evil and sinful. The prophet Jeremiah continued to call on him to repent, which he failed to do. Judah became a vassal of Egypt and was forced to pay a large tribute to its new master. However, when the Babylonians defeated Egypt in 605 BC, they attacked Judah and laid siege to Jerusalem. Judah switched sides to Babylon, where Jehoiakim handed over not only taxes and tribute but hostages and items from the Temple.

Jehoiakim thought he would again play the great powers off each other when, after Babylon failed in an attempt to invade Egypt in 601 BC, Judah again switched sides and failed to pay Babylon its promised tribute. Nebuchadnezzar II invaded Judah and besieged Jerusalem. Judah was defeated, Jerusalem and the Temple were looted, and its last two kings became Babylonian puppets who continued to ignore the prophet Jeremiah. In 587 BC, the last king, Zedekiah, attempted to rebel against Babylon by again engaging in diplomatic power politics by allying with Egypt. This time, the Babylonians returned, destroyed the city and the Temple, and ushered in the Babylonian captivity. This ended any semblance of an independent Jewish nation on earth.

Although the captivity was harsh, it is speculated that the Jews learned skills from the Babylonians that would come to the fore later, such as banking, commerce, and trade.

In 539 BC, Persia defeated Babylon and became the great power of the age. By royal decree, Cyrus (2 Chronicles, Ezra, Isaiah, Daniel) saved the Jewish people from both assimilation and destruction. Darius I (Ezra, Nehemiah, Daniel, Haggai, Zechariah) took steps that would forever shift history, not only by rebuilding the Temple, but by pushing the Jews to be ruled no longer by a monarchy but by a high priest.

This Persian period illustrates the third typology of international affairs for the Jews, the so-called Persian model where the Jewish people allied themselves with greater imperial power in exchange for autonomy but not independence. Persia, for its part, desiring imperial stability, wanted the Jews to accept a single Torah and believed the rebuilding of the Temple would add to both their political and religious stability, making their rule easier. This was especially noted during the rule of the Persian king Artaxerxes (465–424 BC).

It was during the Persian period (Ezra, Nehemiah) that we see the emergence of the Sadducees, an upper-echelon priestly class devoted to the Temple. They believed in the literal interpretation of the Torah and rejected the idea of an afterlife. However, as this Temple was recognized as being sponsored by a foreign power, its legitimacy would continue to be questioned. Thus, it was the Persians who propelled the Temple and the priests to rule, as they had no desire to re-create a Jewish monarchy, especially not one modeled on David and Solomon. This would set the stage for a conflict between the Sadducees and the Pharisees. Because the Sadducees were created by a foreign power, it is interesting that they would be destroyed by another foreign power, the Romans. The Sadducees were also the group more attracted to foreign assimilation, especially during the Hellenization era. Their obsession with the Temple would prove their undoing.

Athenian Empire

Greece, unlike many ancient kingdoms, was not a united concept. It was a series of city-states, the most important of which was Athens, though Athens itself is not mentioned in the Bible until the New Testament in Acts and 1 and 2 Thessalonians. Although the Athenian state mirrored most ancient societies with a king and land-owning aristocracy, this began to change. In 594 BC, it embraced the constitution created by Solon, which began the foundations of Athenian democracy. Athens went through a period of tyrants that undermined Solon's reforms until the statesman Cleisthenes solidified democracy in 510 BC. The wars with Persia began in 499 BC, which also gave rise to a great Athenian empire, dispelling a common myth in contemporary international relations that democracies are not inherently empire builders. One must keep in mind that when the Athenians went to war, they did so not only by voting, but by voting for themselves to engage in battle. The on-again, off-again enemy of Athens was Sparta, but Sparta never had the international affairs impact that Athens did.

The Persian Wars that liberated the Jews were also the wars that would lead not only to the downfall of the Persians but the conquest of Israel by the Greeks. Due to the Persian Wars, Athens formed the Delian League of 150 city-states, which became the most powerful force in the Mediterranean. It cleared out Persian control by 465 BC as Athens dominated trade and commerce with a strong navy and merchant fleet.

From 431 BC to 401 BC, Greece descended into the most important conflict for international relations of that age, the Peloponnesian War. It was during this time that the famous Melian Dialogue took place, which birthed the entire school of realism in international relations.

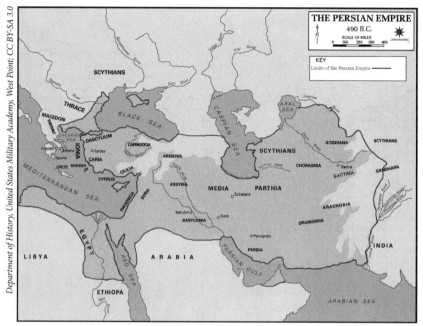

Figure 2-19: Persian Empire, 499 BC

In 416 BC, Athens demanded the surrender of Melos for purely political and economic means, Melos refused, and Athens destroyed it. The weakness caused by the conflict led to the eventual conquest of Greece and the defeat of Athens in 338 BC by the Kingdom of Macedon, first by Philip II and solidified by his son Alexander.

The period of the Persian and Peloponnesian wars witnessed the rise of Greek philosophy in the Socratic, Platonic, and Aristotelian fashion. All three philosophical schools contributed to natural law, universal law, and morality ideas that would impact international relations. This Greek period becomes immensely important when discussing the Hellenization conflict in the Old Testament and, conversely, the use of these ideas by St. Paul in his conversion of the Gentiles in the New Testament.

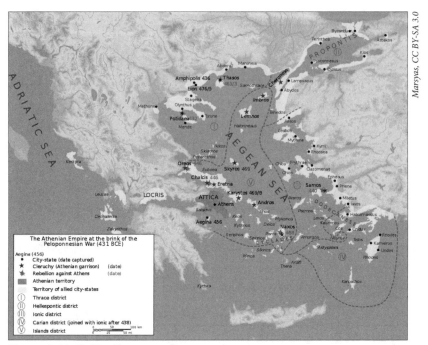

Figure 2-20: Delian League

Thus, the Greeks ushered in one of the great pivot points in international affairs, the ramification of which would be hard to measure. The Greco-Persian Wars determined the fate not only of the Greeks and Persians but also the Jews, the Romans, and even American civilization. In fact, one could argue that had the Persians succeeded, not only would Western civilization been deferred, but it is quite possible there would have been no American civilization that would be recognizable today.

In 499 BC, under Cyrus I, Persia had backed tyrants in its Greek provinces in Asia Minor. The blowback of this caused the Ionian Revolt, which brought the Athenian democratic empire to aid their fellow Greeks and put Greece on a collision course with the Persian Empire.

In 490 BC, when Darius I was king, the Persian army met a primarily Athenian force of about ten thousand who were outnumbered by a

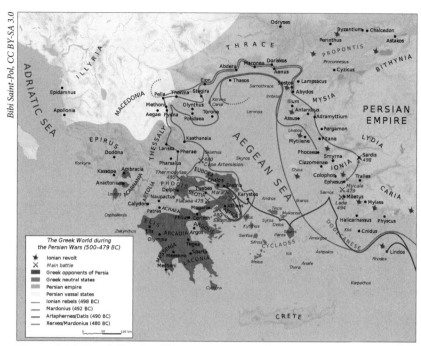

Figure 2-21: Greek Persian Wars

huge ratio (estimates range from 3 and 10 to 1). The Athenians defeated the Persians. The Persians were expelled from Europe, only to return in 480 BC under King Xerxes, where the famous three hundred Spartans held them at bay at Thermopylae. This led to the Persians' ultimate defeat at the Battle of Salamis, which ended Persian influence in Europe and the Mediterranean and would lead directly to its eventual downfall and the rise of Alexander the Great (356–323 BC) of Macedon. Alexander's victories against the Persian Empire, especially his capture of what is today Syria, Lebanon, and Israel in 333 and 332 BC, changed the face of biblical history completely. It was the Hellenization and colonization by the Greek Gentiles that would set the stage for the climactic events of the later Old Testament and New Testament.

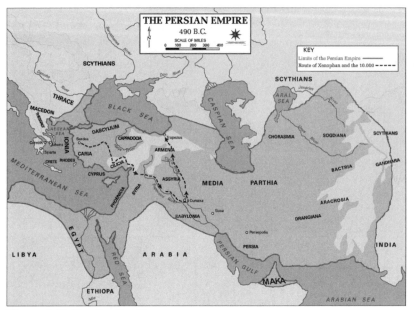

Figure 2-22: Persian Empire

One can illustrate it this way: the Greeks, especially Athenian victories at Marathon and Salamis, would launch the Athenian Empire to new heights, causing the friction with Sparta that would create the Peloponnesian War. This war allowed Alexander to solidify his control over Greece and create an empire that would plant Gentile communities across the region. There would be no Seleucid (Greek) dynasty for the Maccabees to revolt against without this action. Further, there also would have been no indigenous Gentile community to conflict with the Jews during the Roman occupation without these events.

Hellenization

The issue of Hellenization was intertwined with the story of Alexander the Great, born in 356 BC and died in 323 BC. Hellenization was the process that spread Greek language, culture, religion, and ideas

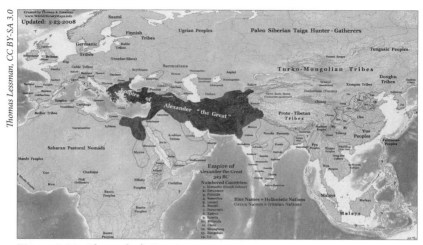

Figure 2-23: Alexander's Empire

throughout the world, which followed the conquests of Alexander and his empire.

In 336 BC, Alexander took the kingship of Macedon after his father had been assassinated. In 334 BC, he began his conquest of the Persian Empire and reached Egypt by 332 BC. By 327 BC, he had conquered Persia and moved on to India. Alexander, theoretically, was a hereditary monarch who ruled through appointed leaders. He established cities that became centers of Greek life and population such as Alexandria in Egypt. However, Alexander had not named a successor when he died in 323 BC. This broke his empire up among his generals.

The empire was divided among four generals who spent much of their time fighting each other. Important from a biblical perspective was Ptolemy I, who established the Ptolemaic dynasty, and Seleucus I Nicator, who established the Seleucid dynasty. These two would vie for control over Israel.

The Hellenization of Israel and the reaction against it serves as one of the most telling aspects of the Old Testament and international relations. The Jews, who had been favored subjects of the Persians, would

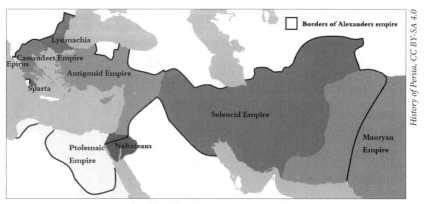

History of Persia, CC BY-SA 4.0

Figure 2-24: Division of Alexander's Empire

now fall under the Greek world. This led to the establishment of larger Gentile colonies, which were often populated by Greek veterans, such as a colony of Macedonians who settled in Samaria. It also created Greek cities, temples, and culture and a flood of goods from the Greek world. The Greeks set up a system of tax farming contracts among the wealthy natives who would then be responsible for collecting taxes and living off the excess. This would later be copied by the Romans in the form of the infamous publicans.

The Jews adopted many aspects of high Greek culture and language. The common word for a Jewish house of worship, "synagogue," was also from the Greek. The powerful Jewish Sanhedrin, the high religious tribunal and administrative council, was based on the Greek Synhedrion or Greek Council, which appeared in the fourth century BC and was not part of the Old Testament. Yet this too would be a pivotal issue in the New Testament as the Sanhedrin tried to persecute Jesus.

Great power conflict in international relations again determined the fate of the people of Israel. They were caught between two Greek empires as a result of Alexander's death: the Seleucids to their north with their capital in Syria and the Ptolemies to their south, who were headquartered in Egypt. The back and forth of conquest and reconquest over Israel continued at least five times. It was during this Hellenized time that the high priest of the Temple became the central point of governance over the Jews.

Hellenization caused great fissures in Judaism at this time. Conservative Jewish society was appalled at the Greek paganism, the nudity of the Greek gymnasiums and athletic contests, and Greek attitudes about morality.

Much of Israel was ruled over by the Seleucids by 198 BC. It was during this time that the tradition of the high priest of the Temple, which had primarily been passed from father to son, was changed so that it became a position appointed by the foreign political ruler, who determined who was high priest and who therefore would be head of the Sanhedrin. Thus, Antiochus IV, who ruled from 175 BC to 164 BC, deposed the conservative high priest Onias III in 175 BC in favor first of Jason and then later Menelaus, who advocated the Hellenization of Judaism.

Thus, by the time we get to the New Testament, a foreign-inspired group, the Sanhedrin, try Jesus, motivated by the foreign-appointed high priest, Caiaphas, neither of which is justified by the Old Testament. This is international relations at play.

There was growing suspicion and resentment that came to a head when the Seleucid ruler Antiochus IV entered and despoiled the Temple in 168 BC. Antiochus had a campaign to expunge the Jewish faith, ban the Torah, and establish Greek religious practices. An example of this Hellenization run amok was that many Jewish youths were attracted to the Greek lifestyle and culture, even abandoning Hebrew.

However, none of this would have happened without the role of the great powers, and here is where a new player emerges, Rome. Republican Rome was an ally of the Ptolemies in Egypt. Antiochus wanted to assert control over Egypt. He launched multiple wars but was always afraid of angering the Romans. The despoiling of the Temple occurred as Antiochus was humiliated by Rome on his way back from Egypt in one of the most famous events in the history of international relations, which becomes known as the red line.

The story out of antiquity shows a single Roman consul, Gaius Popillius Laenas, alone with his two clerks facing the might of the Seleucid Empire, which was threatening the Roman protectorate of Egypt in 168 BC. The old consul's mission was to force the king to return to Syria. The exchange between the two, as the story itself, has many variations. However, they all boil down to the following: The king, laughing at the *diktat* issued by the Roman, asks the classic version of you and what army is going to force me back to Syria away from Egypt. The Roman responds by drawing a circle in the sand and saying that when he steps across the line, he had better be marching toward Syria and not Egypt. The Seleucid king, realizing that this old man and his line represented the might of Rome, retreated, and the red line concept was born. The concept of a red line in international relations is now in vogue to describe a situation where one nation or coalition sets up a trip wire that, if crossed, will result in a dire consequence. It should be interesting to readers how history comes full circle since the last time the term "red line" became famous was over President Barack Obama's use of the concept in dealing with none other than the dictatorship of Syria.

Thus, the Roman intervention, one can argue, indirectly sparked the Maccabean Revolt in 164 BC and the establishment of the Jewish Hasmonean dynasty, which would later be replaced by the same Romans.

The Maccabean Revolt was led by Mattathias, who was both a landowner and priest who opposed the Hellenization of the Jews. He and his insurgents fled to the Judean Hills, where he died in 166 BC and was replaced by his son Judas Maccabeus, and then in succession his surviving brothers. The war between them and the Seleucid Empire continued back and forth until accommodation was made with Simon, the last surviving brother, in 142 BC when he was named high priest and prince of Israel. It was his son, John Hyrcanus (ruled from 134 BC to 104 BC), who became the first Hasmonean king (ethnarch) of Israel and high priest, even though neither office fit the biblical conditions of lineage.

The Old Testament and International Relations

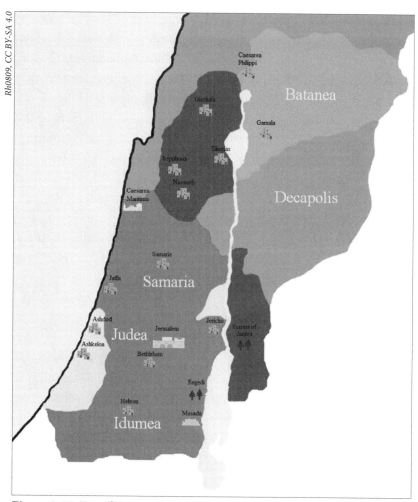

Rh0809, CC BY-SA 4.0

Figure 2-25: Era of Roman Republic

The Hasmoneans expanded their power into Judea, Samaria, Idumea, and Galilee; and with it spread their version of Judaism. Hycarnus was able to do this, again due to the great power conflict between the dying Seleucids and the rising Parthians. However, this also created a rift where Jews from these outer areas were never considered 100 percent Jewish. This was uniquely the case with Galilee, which would become the epicenter of early Christianity. These wars against fellow Jews were quite brutal, as demonstrated by Hyrcanus's attack on Samaria in 113 BC, where he destroyed the Samaritan temple on Mount Gerizim and brutally forced the conversion of the people of Idumea (Edomites). He successfully established good diplomatic relations with the Roman Republic, gaining the support of the Roman Senate and good relations with Egypt. Upon the death of Hyrcanus, a Hasmonean civil war erupted at the top involving Hyrcanus's sons and wife, who he named regent but who was killed (starved to death) by her eldest son, Aristobulus I. Aristobulus took power and called himself Basileus, a Greek word indicating something akin to an emperor. He died in 103 BC, and a further division occurred with the remaining brothers, including the machinations and interventions of foreign powers like the remaining Seleucids and Nabateans (Arabians).

The most crucial biblical event of this time was probably in 250 BC, when the Jews of Alexandria, who may have made up 40 percent of the population, translated the Old Testament into Greek.

This was also the era of great conflict between the Sadducees and the Pharisees (as well as the Essenes, who played no role in international affairs). If the Sadducees were the party of assimilation and the upper class, the Pharisees were the party of the general public, believing in both the written and oral tradition of Judaism, an afterlife, and the concept of a Messiah. Most famous regarding the issue of international affairs, they were not interested in assimilation and were upset with the forced conversions committed by the Hasmoneans. They became a more critical and distinct group during the Maccabean Revolt. The Pharisees were a combination of scholar and priest who opposed the attitudes and actions of the Sadducees and encouraged a life centered not around the single Temple of Jerusalem but in synagogues everywhere.

This all came to a head when the people of Israel experienced, for the first time, a female regent ruler, Salome Alexander, who ruled from 76 BC to 67 BC with her son Hyrcanus II as high priest. His younger brother, Aristobulus II, rebelled and threw the nation into chaos and violence. The Sadducees supported Aristobulus II, while the Pharisees backed Hyrcanus II. These two groups essentially devolved into political partisans. There was some reconciliation between 67 BC and 63 BC, which could have ended the people of Israel's foreign tribulations had it not been for the intervention of Antipater the Idumenan. Antipater founded the future Herodians and was the father of Herod I. He used suspicions, foreign involvement, and paranoia to reignite the civil war and violence. This resulted in both brothers appealing to Rome for support by pleading to the Roman general Marcus Scaurus, who had taken possession of Syria from the Seleucids. This final civil war was ended only by Roman intervention by Pompey the Great in 63 BC, who was frustrated with all Jewish sides. When these factions attempted to resist Rome, Pompey became even more aggravated. This led to his decision to take Jerusalem, enter the Temple, and incorporate what would now be known as Judea into the province of Syria. The words of Josephus about this are illuminating: "For this misfortune which befell Jerusalem, Hyrcanus and Aristobulus were responsible."

Rome was now master of the people of Israel.

CHAPTER 3

The International Relations of the Roman Republic and the New Testament

For nation shall rise against nation, and kingdom against kingdom:
and there shall be famines, and pestilences, and earthquakes,
in divers places.

—MATTHEW 24:7

Four hundred years pass between the end of the Old Testament and the beginning of the New Testament. The Hellenistic period and the Maccabean Revolt are not in the King James Bible, but they are critical to understanding the international relations of the Bible. Many Christians term this period the intertestamental time. The period from the Hasmonean civil war to the destruction of the Temple was one dominated by the Romans in international relations. The entire New Testament revolves around Jesus, who is born, lives, dies, and is resurrected during Roman rule. It is, therefore, impossible to explain the international relations, foreign policy, and diplomacy of this period without a complete understanding of the Roman rule.

Just as the Bible is divided into the Old and New Testament, the Roman period in the Bible covers the late republican period that stretches from 509 BC, when Romans overthrew their kings, to 27 BC, when Octavian, later Augustus (Luke 2:1, Acts 25: 21-25, Acts 27:1), became princeps (First Citizen). From Augustus onward, Rome was put on a path of rulership by a succession of emperors. However, one should not confuse the Roman imperial period, which is dated from 27 BC to 476 AD, to Rome's empire building. The Roman Empire began under the republic, just as democratic Athens had engaged in empire building. Greek empire building ultimately resulted in Israel falling into the Hellenized world. Republican Rome built an empire as well, and it was during this late republican period that Rome exerted influence and eventual control over Judea.

The Roman Republic

Three factors led to the Romans entering Jerusalem. The first was the Hasmonean civil war, where both sides invited them in to restore order against the other; the second was the Seleucid dissolution; and finally, the rise of Parthia.

This work will not attempt to illustrate the entirety of the Roman Republic, but it will offer insights to explain the international relations backdrop to the Bible and Rome's role. Rome endured a regal period from 753 to 509 BC, when it overthrew its last monarch and established the Republic. Rome battled with moral realism versus realism in the manner that American history battled and continues to battle between liberalism and realism. Although Rome was often brutal, rapacious, and militaristic, it was also very concerned about its word and its treaty obligations. It inherited and evolved Greek concepts about universal and natural law, with Roman senators and philosophers like Cicero writing:

> There is indeed a law, right reason, which is in accordance with nature; existing in all, unchangeable, eternal. Commanding us to do what is right, forbidding us to do what is wrong. It has dominion over good men, but possesses no influence over bad

ones. No other law can be substituted for it, no part of it can be taken away, nor can it be abrogated altogether...but it is eternal and immutable for all nations and for all time.

This belief was combined with Roman stoicism concerning honesty and duty. It had intense internal debates about *fides* and *pietas* and the need to have declared and legal wars, not just organized violence.

The republican period was marked by Rome's territorial expansion, and Rome emerged as the primary Italian state by 275 BC. It fought a bipolar conflict with the Carthaginians over dominance of the Mediterranean during the Punic Wars from 264 BC to 146 BC. The republican period was dominated by the domestic struggle between the two social orders (referred to as the struggle of the orders) in Rome, the upperclass patricians and the lower-class plebeians. It adopted an ancient constitution of sorts when it created the Twelve Tables in 451 BC.

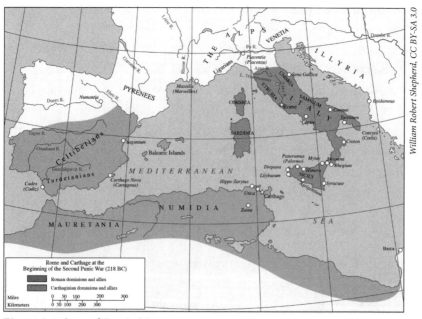

Figure 3-1: Second Punic War

It is believed that the Roman Senate, the organism of the patricians, existed earlier than the Republic and was the premiere Roman institution either in reality or symbolically for Rome's entire history. Americans need to differentiate the Roman Senate, which played such a key role over events concerning Israel (Judea), from the American Senate. The Roman Senate could only offer advice, but that advice had close to the rule of law due to the esteem of the institution. It, however, controlled money and generally managed foreign affairs.

During the early Republic, there were two plebian assemblies for civilian and military affairs. As early as the sixth century BC, Rome's primary political position was the annually elected dual consuls. The primary job of the consuls was to act as main military commanders of the Roman army, which was made up entirely of property-owning Roman male citizens. This was the case unless there was a military crisis, in which case a temporary dictator for six months was chosen to deal with the situation. During the republican period, offices that appear in the Bible were created. The best prize during both the republican and imperial periods was governor (legate) of a province, reserved for the senatorial class, until the imperial period. Provinces that had been pacified earlier were senatorial provinces such as Greece, while provinces acquired later were imperial provinces under the personal thumb of the emperor like Egypt, Syria, and Judea. These governors were often former consuls and thus held the title of proconsul, and they held supreme military and civil power in a province. Quirinius (Luke 2:2) of the New Testament was an example of this. The governor's word was law, and only an appeal to the Senate, and later the emperor, could countermand him. Good governors provided Rome with stability and profit while keeping their respective populaces happy or at least pacified. Bad governors, as Pliny the Younger demonstrated, were engaged in corruption and brutality, and some were indicted for various crimes such as extortion and embezzlement.

A prefect was often the chief subordinate to a governor and thus acted as a governor of a specific region. This was the role of Pontius Pilate.

A praetor was an officer in the provinces who had judicial and political power. The office is mentioned collectively in the book of Acts, Chapter 16. They were often the senior Roman magistrate in an area. A quaestor had financial administrative power, and a censor monitored the lists of people and property. Military offices and duties will be dealt with in the next chapter, but they play an equally critical role in the New Testament.

Rome's victory against Carthage, after over one hundred years of war, was the catalyst that brought Rome into the lands of the Bible. Only after victory and its total destruction of Carthage did Rome move eastward from the Mediterranean basin, swallowing the Hellenized world, dividing the Western world into provinces run by governors and prefects, and garrisoning the empire with Roman and auxiliary soldiers. Although Rome allied with the Greeks, it made Greece into a protectorate by 194 BC. The impact of their interaction and ultimate conquest of the Greek world was to fuse Greco-Roman religion and philosophy in law, art, literature, architecture, and lifestyle.

Roman foreign policy toughened by 170 BC, and it conquered the Mediterranean basin by 130 BC. In 129 BC, Rome created a new aristocratic class that affected the story of Jesus, when the *ordo equester*, or *equites*, were created. These equestrian knights, one of whom was Pontius Pilate, ranked right below senators and were often the backbone of Roman administration. The *equites* were a good match for being a prefect. It should be noted that these administrators were the gritty side of the aristocracy, the aristocrats who had to work their way up the military and political ladder. Their aristocratic lineage gave them keys to doors that could otherwise not be opened, but they had to prove themselves in ways the patrician senatorial class did not. As Rome expanded, it gained more revenue from her provinces; this required more soldiers, whose duty became more one of pacification. As Alexander had Hellenized the biblical world, Rome would Romanize it.

In 107 BC, Rome instituted the Marian reforms in the army that created the bedrock of the professional military system, open to all Roman male citizens and foreign allied auxiliaries.

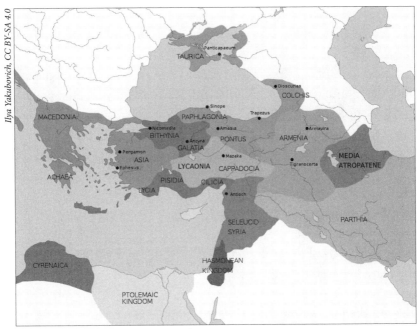

Figure 3-2: Rome versus Mithridates

Pompey (106 BC–48 BC), known as Pompey the Great, who had been consul, was given the job to rid the Mediterranean of ancient terrorists, the pirates. An event in 66 BC proved pivotal to all future biblical events. Pompey was given command of the Roman army to fight against King Mithridates of Pontus and Armenia. His victory led to Rome taking over the biblical lands and turning Syria into a province of Rome, Romanizing the east.

The late republican period was one of civil strife and civil war. In 60 BC, the First Triumvirate (three leaders), whose members had all been powerful consuls and military leaders, was created with Licinius Crassus, Julius Caesar, and Pompey. Pompey was defeated by Caesar in 48 BC and was assassinated in Egypt. One of Julius Caesar's policies was to expand the system of settling army veterans in colonies as well as expanding into Asia Minor and the modern Middle East. In 44 BC,

Julius Caesar, who had filled the power vacuum created by this period to become dictator, was assassinated, which effectively ended much of the Republic.

Now the Roman world was divided between Octavian (Augustus) and Mark Antony from 42 BC to 31 BC. This stability was temporary, as the two clashed over who would rule the Western world, which culminated in the Battle of Actium in 31 BC. Octavian emerged victorious, becoming Caesar Augustus.

The religion of the Republic was the pagan religion inherited from the Greeks, whose mythology was Romanized. Foreign cults such as Mithraism and powerful philosophic ideas—in particular stoicism, which preached a life of duty, honor, obligation, responsibility, and a sober view of death—permeated the fabric of Roman life. How serious the patrician class took the mythological aspects of Roman religion is up for considerable debate, although history judges it was more of a cultural demonstration than a deeply spiritual experience. They were tolerant of foreign religions, the clash of which was not dramatically illustrated until the creation of the emperor's cult during the rule of the emperors, starting in 42 BC when the Roman Senate declared Julius Caesar divine.

The Romans created the first globalized economy based on trade and proto-industrialization. Much of the economy was borne on the backs of the slaves and farmers. Grain in particular was critical, and provinces like Egypt and routes such as those through Judea were critical to Rome's survival. Trade routes extended as far as China for silk, Western Europe for metal and gems, and India for spice. The land routes were protected by Roman soldiers who traveled by Roman roads, and the Roman navy patrolled the waterways.

Parthia

Parthia (Acts 2:9), a term representing modern Iran, had been a province under Alexander the Great's empire and thus had been taken over

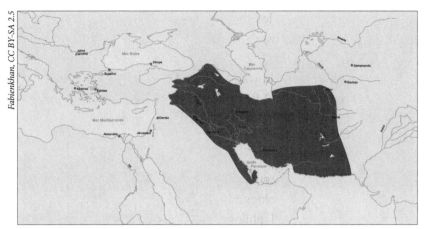

Figure 3-3: Parthian Empire

by the Seleucids. War broke out between the declining Seleucid state and the rising Parthians around 238 BC. War and civil strife continued as the Parthians were able to take control of greater Persia (Iran); by about 190 BC, they had finally defeated the Seleucids. Parthia began expanding its empire, especially under the aforementioned King Mithridates (171–132 BC). Parthia's religious views were a combination of Persian and Hellenistic elements, and it created a trading and commercial empire similar to the Roman Republic.

The Parthians always faced foreign threats, to their east from nomadic tribes from China and to their west from the increasingly powerful Roman Republic. However, they also controlled the overland trade routes between China and enjoyed good diplomatic relations with Han dynasty China. In the first century BC, the Indo-Parthian Kingdom was created, incorporating areas such as modern Afghanistan and Pakistan. War broke out numerous times between Parthia and Rome, even though they had agreed that the Euphrates River would be the recognized boundary.

One of the continuous sticking points between the two empires was the Kingdom of Armenia. Both empires wanted it as a buffer state

Figure 3-4: Roman Parthian War

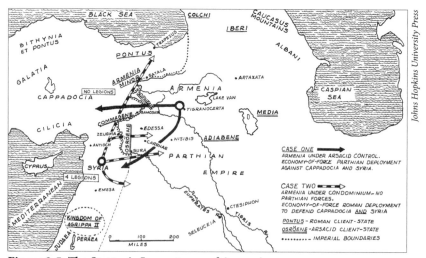

Figure 3-5: The Strategic Importance of Armenia

between each other, and both wanted to be the primary influence in the kingdom. Armenia's proximity to Syria and Judea made such arrangements critical to our understanding of the international relations issue in the region.

Figure 3-6: Parthian Invasion

In 53 BC, the Roman proconsul of Syria, one of the Triumvirate, went to war against Parthia and was defeated at the Battle of Carrhae. The Parthians then invaded Roman territory in Syria.

The biblical lands changed hands between Parthia and Rome, and they were caught up not only in the Roman-Parthian conflict but also in Rome's civil wars following the assassination of Julius Caesar. In 40 BC, Antigonus, the second son of Aristobulus II, returned to Judea, and with Parthian help, attempted to seize control of it. The pro-Roman Jewish forces in Jerusalem, led by High Priest Hyrcanus II and Herod the Idumean (later the Great) for example, were defeated by Parthia and her Jewish allies. Hyrcanus was carried off to Babylon, where he was mutilated so he could no longer hold the position of high priest. Herod fled Jerusalem.

In 40 BC, Antigonus was placed as high priest by the Parthians, and Herod fled to Rome to appeal to the Roman Senate, who heard his pleas and appointed him king. Here, biblical history was forever changed. Herod becomes king because of the international relations battle between the superpowers of the first century BC, Parthia and Rome. Herod had backed the right horse in Rome, and Rome would reward him with the Jewish throne. Herod and his Roman allies, under the leadership of Mark Antony, fought until he became king in 37 BC. Parthia and Rome would vie for dominance and meddle in others affairs during the entire period of the New Testament. However, one among many reasons that Rome wanted control over Judea was its proximity to and potential buffer from the Parthian threat.

Judea

Before this, Pompey had acquired Judea and had appointed Hyrcanus as high priest. In 57 BC, the Roman governor of Syria, Aulus Gabininus, split Judea into three districts: Galilee, Samaria, and Judea. Judea was governed by five to ten Sanhedrin councils, Jerusalem, home of the Great Sanhedrin, being one of them. In an unexpected move, Hyrcanus sided with Julius Caesar in his war with Pompey, even sending Jewish troops to Alexandria, Egypt, to support Caesar. In 47 BC, he was rewarded for this by being made *ethnarch* (a Greek word meaning ethnic tribal chief) of Judea. Antipater, the Idumean, became procurator. His son, Herod, took over the administration of Galilee; and his other son, Phasael, the administration of Jerusalem. Herod ingratiated himself with Roman officials, especially the governor of Syria, who heaped on him greater responsibility and power. It should be noted, even at this early time, the Jewish religious upper class saw him as brutal and unrestrained.

Much of the interplay between the international relations of Judea, and especially between Judea and Rome, focuses on the personage of Herod I. Herod was born in 73 BC and died in 4 BC. He was from Idumea, and thus an Edomite, so his Judaism was always suspect. Thus, where he was born added to his illegitimacy, as did his negative personal habits and morals. His father, Antipater, was favored by Julius Caesar. After proving himself in Galilee, Herod and his brother Phasael

Figure 3-7: Israel Under the Maccabees

were named tetrarchs by Mark Antony when Judea was embroiled in the Roman civil war and the Roman-Parthian wars. As previously mentioned, Herod fled to Rome, got himself named king by the Roman

Senate, and retook Judea by 37 BC, ushering in the Herodian dynasty in Jewish history. The last of the Hasmonean princes was Aristobulus III, whose mother was friends with Cleopatra, who had married Mark Antony. This placed Herod in the unenviable position of triangulating the situation in Rome, Egypt, and Judea in order to stay in power. He killed this last Hasmonean, earning him the enmity of Egypt's ruler. He further made the mistake of choosing the wrong side in the Roman civil war between Antony (and Cleopatra) and Octavian (later using the name Augustus).

The IR world changed in 31 BC due to the Battle of Actium, where Octavian triumphed. It secured the Roman Empire for the Julio-Claudian dynasty, changing Rome into an imperial monarchy and becoming the reigning superpower on the planet. Herod ventured to the island of Rhodes to meet with Augustus and convince him of his loyalty. It is believed he did this by promising stability and the ability to defend the Judean frontiers from Rome's enemies. Here again, IR plays a critical role. Rome was very concerned about Parthian incursions, and a stable and loyal ruler in Judea would be important. Herod's rule depended on Rome; the vitality of the Roman Empire became his cause.

Herod (Matthew, Mark, Luke, Acts) is one of the most infamous people in the New Testament, second only to Judas Iscariot. He was, like many rulers, seen in a dual light. His material contributions were enormous, such as the rebuilding of the Temple (including the Temple Mount) as well as constructing the fortress at Masada, the port at Caesarea Maritima, and the city of Sebaste (primarily for the Gentile population). He fed the poor during times of need. In this sense, Herod was "the Great."

On the other hand, he is forever blemished by his massacre of the innocents. According to Matthew 2:16:

> Then Herod, when he saw that he was mocked of the wise men, was exceeding wroth, and sent forth, and slew all the children that were in Bethlehem, and in all the coasts thereof, from two

years old and under, according to the time which he had diligently inquired of the wise men.

This single act alone condemns him to history. Subsequently, Joseph escaped with Mary and Jesus to the sanctuary in Egypt. Egypt was beyond Herod's reach yet still within the boundaries of the Roman Empire.

His lack of commitment to the Jewish faith played a pivotal rule in the Bible. He lived the life of a libertine, engaging in outlandish spending and, in an effort to curry favor with Rome, placing a golden eagle at the top of the Temple. Further, he was exceptionally brutal—he created a secret police, engaged in harsh taxation measures, and had to rely on foreign mercenaries from places like Thracia (southeastern Europe), Germania (Germany), and Gaul (France).

Herod died, probably in 4 BC, when Jesus was a little child. Between the multiple executions of various family members and his inability to name a single successor, his will, which Augustus observed, divided Judea into a tetrarchy of three ethnarchs, Herod Antipas being one of them. This continued until 6 AD, when most of Judea became a Roman province except for Galilee and Perea, which were ruled by Herod Antipas, infamous as well in the New Testament.

A word about how the Romans viewed themselves is in order. Two Roman virtues abound. The first is expressed in the Latin word *fides*, or good faith. This was the idea of one's honor-bound word. Thus, it was not so much whether something was moral or immoral but whether a person honored an agreement or, in international relations, a treaty or diplomatic arrangement. The second word is *pietas*, which we derive piety from. This, however, goes beyond personal piety and embraces concepts of family honor, obligation, and observance of ritual.

Two Roman stories depict the idealized vision that Romans aspired to become. These stories exemplify the national character of the Romans. One of the most important aspects of international relations is looking at such national character. Americans' national character is often depicted as upholding values such as independence, freedom, liberty, equality, justice, patriotism, and self-reliance. Roman character was noted for exemplifying sternness, diligence, dutifulness, self-sacrifice, and stoicism.

The first story is entitled Horatio at the Bridge. It is the tale of Horatius Cocles, the name Cocles meaning cyclops, as he had become one-eyed from previous battles. The story came from the sixth century BC when a Roman patrician who held a position in the republican army defended the only bridge (Pons Sublicius) across the Tiber River that was a gateway to the city of Rome. As the Roman army was being routed by the invading Etruscans, Horatio led two other soldiers in an almost suicidal defense of the bridge, embarrassing the cowards who had fled to turn back and defend the bridge until it could be destroyed, saving the city. Wounded numerous times, he limped back to the city, where he later retired with a large gift of land, as any good Roman would have wanted. Thus, a hundred years before the three hundred Spartans defended the pass at Thermopylae, the Romans beat them to it with three men.

The second story, which was branded in the mind and soul of George Washington, was that of Cincinnatus.

Lucius Quinctius Cincinnatus was another Roman patrician and more of a historical figure than Horatio. He was born in 519 BC and died in 430 BC. He became the touchstone of Roman virtue. Cincinnatus (the curly haired) was Roman consul in 460 BC when the battles between the class orders were violent and extreme. He retired to his farm after his one-year term. In 458 BC, Rome suffered a complete military disaster against the Aequi, plunging the Roman Senate into chaos and panic. They appointed Cincinnatus dictator for six months. He raised a citizen army, marched against the Aequi, and defeated them in fifteen days. Rather than keep absolute power for the remainder of his term, he promptly resigned and went back to his farm. In 439 BC, in response to one of the plebeian leaders trying to make himself king,

Cincinnatus was again appointed dictator and, after restoring order in twenty-one days, again resigned back to his farm.

The legend is clear: republican virtues are the prime marker of Roman manhood. This extended even to Augustus, who refused to establish a Roman monarchy; although he was emperor, he preferred the title of princeps, or First Citizen. Fifteen hundred years later, this story makes the jump across the Atlantic to the Founding Fathers, especially George Washington, who knowingly saw himself as the American Cincinnatus. Two American cities (in Ohio and New York) are named for the Roman, as is the famous Society of Cincinnatus.

These Roman legends are not merely points of interest. They illustrate the worldview of the Romans in their own idealized vision and thus give us insight into how they ruled the wider world. Many of these values were able to traverse through space and time to form the blueprint of the American government.

CHAPTER 4

The International Relations of the Roman Empire and the New Testament

And it came to pass in those days, that there went out a decree from Caesar Augustus, that all the world should be taxed.

—LUKE 2:1

The New Testament begins under the reign of the first Roman emperor, Augustus, known previously as Octavian. He was the emperor at the time of the birth of Jesus Christ. Augustus ordered the census that brought Mary and Joseph to Bethlehem under the authority of his governor, Quirinius.

Aside from getting a calendar month from his name, Augustus created the underlying international relations conditions for the entire New Testament. Born in 63 BC, he reigned from 27 BC to his death in 14 AD. He created the first global relations system of an enforced world order, known as a Pax (Peace), the Pax Romana. This happened only two other times in world history: the eighteenth and nineteenth centuries, Pax Britannica, and, most importantly to American readers, the Pax Americana from 1945 until today.

Augustus's great uncle was Julius Caesar, but Caesar had named him his adopted son and heir. Augustus, therefore, became the first of the Julio-Claudian emperors. And, perhaps not coincidently, this line would bookend all the events of the Bible, not including Revelations. The Julio-Claudians started with Augustus, followed by Tiberius, Caligula, Claudius, and ending the Julio-Claudian line with Nero. Augustus is considered one of the best Roman emperors, attempting not only to restore and keep legal and military order but moral order as well, such as his war against adultery and calls for the increase of marriage and legitimate children.

At the time of the birth of Jesus, while Augustus was emperor, Rome controlled about one-third of the earth's population of one hundred million, four million of which lived in the city of Rome. There is speculation on the size of Jerusalem, with some figures having it around one hundred thousand to Tacitus's estimate of six hundred thousand. One archaeologist puts the population of Bethlehem at three hundred.

As noted earlier, following his victory against Mark Antony and Cleopatra in 31 BC, Augustus refused to create a monarchy. Instead he created the Principate, which attempted to retain republican institutions, in particular the Roman Senate, where he was merely First Citizen (princeps). It was said Augustus had a fondness for the title imperator, or commander. He kept many of the republican offices and titles for officials intact. Naturally, in reality, Augustus was the first emperor.

Although Rome kept its legionary motto SPQR (*Senātus Populusque Rōmānus*, for the Senate and the People of Rome), Rome's republican empire was transformed into an imperial empire, annexing much of southeast, western, and central Europe; Spain; the Middle East; Asia Minor; and North Africa. In particular, Syria and Judea became Roman provinces. Judea was allowed a client king in the guise of Herod the Great.

It should, however, be noted that at this time Rome suffered one of its biggest military catastrophes, which ended up solidifying an aspect of the international relations system of the time. In 9 AD, the Roman

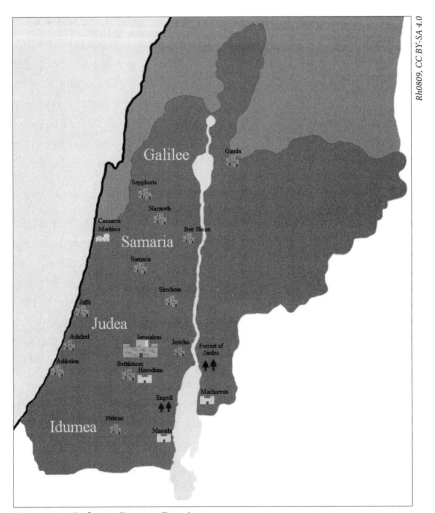

Figure 4-1: Judea as Roman Province

general Publius Varus marched against the Germanic tribes, and his entire army was annihilated, ending the Roman idea of extending the empire into eastern and northeastern Europe. Varus is of particular note since he was governor of Syria prior to Quirinius, who is first mentioned in the book of Luke.

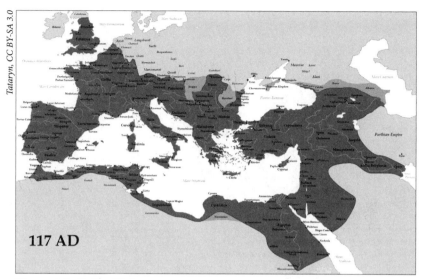

117 AD

Figure 4-2: Buffer States

Emperor Augustus and imperial Rome became the first super-power, and therefore the first superpower to utilize concepts such as vital and national interests to create grand strategy. Rome used both classic realism and moral realism, though it also included peripheral interests by mixing realist goals with Roman concepts of justice and morality.

Augustus formalized a foreign policy of client and buffer states, engaged in complicated diplomacy with Parthia and China, and created the personal army of the emperor (the Praetorian Guard) as well as the police, fire, and postal systems. This was all done alongside a massive expansion of infrastructure (including roads, aqueducts, and ports), trade routes, and a tax system. Further, he stabilized economics, trade, and agriculture. All of this was protected by a standardized professional army. Upon his death, his last words were noted as, "I found Rome a city of clay but left it a city of marble." He was replaced by his adopted son, Tiberius (Luke 3:1).

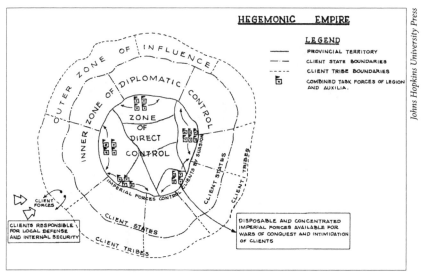

Figure 4-3: Hegemonic Empire

Fundamentally, the international relations conflict of the New Testament is a tale of two cities, Jerusalem and Rome, each with a fundamentally different outlook. For example, from the Roman perspective, a Jew could be a good Roman citizen. The Roman idea of citizenship was much closer to the modern American concept than that of Rome's contemporary neighbors. The importance of this for the Bible is enormous when one contemplates the role of Paul's (Saul's) citizenship, highlighted in particular in the book of Acts. On the other hand, to be Jewish was to be so by birthright, whose spiritual life was dominated by the Temple at Jerusalem, where even those who converted to Judaism or observed it from afar, such as those still living in the places of the Babylonian diaspora, Samaria and Idumea, were at best suspect.

One of the things the Romans and Jews shared was a certainty about their place in the world, a certainty that had to create clash and tension.

For Rome, power was at the center of this certainty, where Rome, the nation, was like a person, a separate entity. The famous Latin phrase, *Dulce et decorum est pro Patria Mori* (it is sweet and fitting to die for

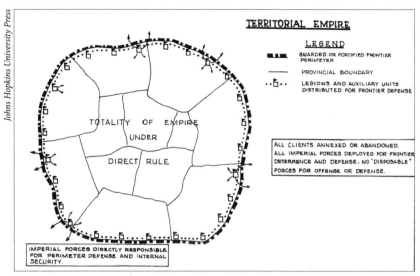

Figure 4-4: Territorial Empire

one's country), emanating from the Roman poet of the time Horace and later taken up by early Christian poets (who Christianized the notion of country), best exemplifies the Roman attitude. The Roman man of virtue was concerned with *res publica* (the public affair)—matters of state and politics. It was a warrior culture that uplifted the Greco-Roman philosophy of stoicism, exemplifying duty, obligation, and responsibility.

On the other hand, the Jerusalem side of the coin was about the centrality of the faith, and that vital location was situated at the Temple. Politically, the Jews shared the notion that the nation was organic; for them, it was the Jewish nation given to them by God, and the highest virtue was obedience to the priests and martyrdom for the faith.

The Roman world was filled with notions of a Roman constitution, which, as the famous Cicero put it, was a combination of monarchy, oligarchy, and democracy. This was a hyper-political society like ancient Athens or the contemporary United States. People battled over political philosophy, ideology, and faction. Life of the elites was dominated by political institutions, especially the Roman Senate, and a universal legal code, often expressed (like America) with lawyers and lawsuits. Jewish thought was dominated by theocracy (we believe Flavius Josephus invented the word itself). Law for the Jews was God-given and expressed in the Torah, in particular the Pentateuch (first five books of the Bible). This was not a world of *res publica* but of religious obedience, where Jewish kings were supposed to be under the prophets and high priests.

Rome's founding was mythological, encompassing the stories of Aeneas (the last Trojan) and Romulus and Remus. Religion was pictured as a pagan divine realm that mirrored the strife of the human world, later dominated by the emperor's cult. It was a religion of evolution with no particular single holy book or beginning where religions and cultural assimilation and syncretism was rife. Rome was, therefore, comfortable melding the emperor's cult, Mithraism, and stoicism. Romans were even willing to make allowances to Judaism and Christianity, but only at the price of observing the emperor's cult. Notably, this was not so much a desire for religious but political domination and fear that those who did not observe the glory of the emperor wanted to revolt.

In stark contrast is the Jewish religion of revelation, of a personal God who is omnipotent, omnipresent, and omniscient, and who demanded no other deity be recognized. It presented the origin of the world clearly in the book of Genesis as a divine plan constructed by a monotheistic God.

In ideological terms, it meant that the conflict between Rome and Jerusalem was inevitable. In practical terms, it meant that the province of Judea would be a unique thorn in Rome's side that could not be ruled exactly as the other provinces were. Further, it resurrected all the old battles of the Maccabees between assimilation into the dominant Roman culture or holding steadfast to Jewish tradition. It is under these international relations terms that Jesus enters the picture when he is made flesh. Jesus represented a clear threat to the entrenched Sanhedrin and a potential threat to Roman stability.

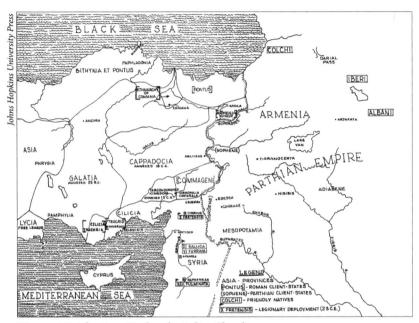

Figure 4-5: The East Under the Julio-Claudians

Roman foreign policy and grand strategy dominated this era in international relations. Rome underwent three grand strategic phases, the last of which was not part of the biblical period. From 300 BC to 66 BC, Rome engaged in a more reactive than preemptive policy and expanded outward during the republican period more organically.

The second phase, which dominates the era of the New Testament, started around 66 BC, around the exact time that Pompey took Jerusalem, to the second century AD, the height of which was around the writing of the book of Acts. This was a hegemonic expansion phase that then settled on territorial integrity and security. The final, extra-biblical phase from the second century AD to the fall of Rome in 476 AD was a defensive phase where Rome attempted to survive as both a nation and an idea. There are many parallels between Roman and American grand strategy, which may be of particular interest to the American reader. Early American grand strategy was based on organic territorial (primarily westward and southern) expansion in its first phase, and then it catapulted into world politics in 1898, entering the stage we live in now from 1945 onward, the Pax Americana.

Rome's imperial statecraft during the biblical period is similar to that of America's. It asked the critical question: How can we maintain a world order system providing for adequate military and diplomatic security while ensuring a prosperous economic base at the same time? In a very interesting parallel to the United States, Rome also needed to do those two things while being able to maintain its political institutions and culture.

It was, therefore, a huge step, just as in the United States, when Rome transitioned from a citizen army to a professional one. Like the United States, there were great fears that this would lead to military rule or military dictatorship and that when Roman male citizens bore less of the military burden, the breakdown of what we today call civil-military relations would occur.

Rome's interest in the provinces was both ideological and utilitarian. It wanted bounty and tribute, commerce and trade, glory and the spread of Roman civilization, and a way to protect territorial integrity.

In another parallel from the American-Soviet Cold War, Rome's only real adversary on the great power stage during biblical times was Parthia. Much of Roman statecraft, including issues over Judea, was dominated by potential or real Parthian actions, just as American foreign policy was equally dominated by Soviet potential or real actions. Thus, when Judea was on the Roman mind, so was Parthia. Just as states like Finland during the Cold War became buffer states between both sides, so did Armenia, which interestingly became the first early kingdom to adopt Christianity as its national religion.

Finally, there is a parallel that Rome's military policy and strategy were subservient to its overall grand strategy. In other words, Rome had very clear strategic interests, and military adventurism would not serve those.

Figure 4-6: The Frontiers in the Second Century

The Julio-Claudians, those who ruled during the New Testament, were particularly aware of the need to conserve and reserve force. They used what modern strategists call a complex strategic toolbox of escalation dominance, coercive diplomacy, and the creation of a hegemonic rather than a purely territorial empire.

This issue of hegemony is important and may also ring similar bells with American strategists. Rome did not need to plant the Roman standard in every place on earth to control the known world. Rather, it needed to create the impression of power beyond the places it directly controlled. Americans went through a similar debate right before the Korean War. Could America engage in perimeter defense (drawing up a fixed boundary and defending all positions on it) or point defense (targeting specific locations of importance)? The United States and Rome could never engage in perimeter defense. Rome created a three-typology system of client states, client tribes, and buffer states.

Figure 4-7: Ancient Trade Routes

The use of client states was exemplified in biblical kingdoms such as Syria-Judea and Egypt. These were considered more advanced by the Romans than the Germanic, British, and Gallic barbarians. These client states were ruled by client monarchs like King Herod, who were expected to ensure tribute, keep domestic order, and be the first line of defense against foreign enemy attacks on the Roman Empire, such as from Parthia. These clients were to ensure Roman border security. The Roman army could not provide perimeter defense, serving as a glorified police force watching every frontier. Rome needed her legions to be mobile; legion mobility became the opposite of perimeter defense, where legions could respond where they were needed or pre-positioned to known hot spots. Client states provided what grand strategic thinkers call strategic depth. Thus, their client rulers were evaluated on how well they maintained foreign and domestic order. The Roman army could only intervene if Roman resources or assets were at stake, or if the client king could not maintain order properly. This is absolutely critical for understanding Roman actions during the New Testament.

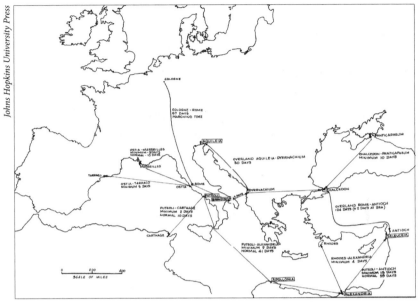

Figure 4-8: Strategic Mobility in the Roman Empire

In Europe, Rome primarily relied on client tribes that were driven to take positive action on behalf of Rome for rewards, or *beneficiat* (modern word: "benefit"). Rome often used larger demonstrations of force here since the population was considered more primitive and needed more overt force to convey Rome's power and message.

Herod again provides the best example of this system in the east. He was Rome's client king and was expected to maintain order and collect taxes. Rome was not interested in Herod's delusions of grandeur, and he was severely reprimanded by Rome when he, without Roman permission, attacked Nabataea (Arabia) in 32 BC. Thus, Herod's problem with the Jewish population, his growing paranoia and murders, the killing of his sons, and the general discord of his court were all seen by Rome as a problem to its grand strategy.

Rome rarely went on violent binges or expanded for expansion's sake. Rome entrusted its engineers with making psychological imprints on potential adversaries through the slow advance of building bridges, aqueducts, roads, walls, milecastles, outposts, and fortified camps wherever her legions traveled. Rome was also adept at psyops, or psychological operations. An example comes out of Judea during the Great Revolt, which would lead to the Great Diaspora. From 72 to 73 AD, the Romans laid siege to the Jewish fort at Masada. The Jews of today celebrate the heroic last stand and suicide of its defenders as a significant event of martyrdom and are recognized as such in modern Israel. The Roman view was quite different. Rome knew that Masada had no military value and was well aware that the battle would be draining on both time and resources, but it would still expend power to crush the small number of rebels to create the impression that no rebellion of any kind would be tolerated.

The Roman military is key to understanding international relations and the biblical picture. The Roman army of the New Testament era was a professional army. During the early years of the Republic, the Roman military had been a force of four legions (2,500 men per legion) of property owners that had grown into the most celebrated military machine of the age, perhaps of all history save for that of the modern American military. The imperial army was an aggressive force, best suited for offense. Its long-serving veterans were governed by a mind-boggling bureaucracy only common to modern readers. The loyalty of the army was to the emperor, who tried to foster that loyalty by granting large cash bonuses and land grants to retiring veterans. These veterans also served a very real security role, as they were the backbone of Roman colonies abroad. This ready-trained militia could be called up as an instrument of strategic control and stability in areas beyond the immediate reach of the legions.

Emperors feared overly popular military commanders and governors, which is one reason they were frequently rotated. The army was designed to protect Roman frontiers with a vast network of fortifications, instill fear with punitive expeditions, and project Roman power both physically and symbolically. United States foreign policy of the late nineteenth and early twentieth century was a parallel in some ways.

The Roman army of the biblical period was also organized into legions, which in theory had six thousand men divided into ten cohorts. Each cohort had six centuries commanded by a centurion. Thus, each centurion commanded, in theory, a century, or a hundred men.

The backbone of this entire system, so critical to understanding key events in the New Testament, was the office of the centurion. Modern scholars have attempted to translate this military and civil office into contemporary ranks, and some have suggested that a sergeant major is the correct correlation. This fails on many levels, as centurions had military power more common to a captain or a major in the American Army and civil power often of a senior secretary and magistrate. They could come from the lower classes if they proved themselves and could be made a centurion by the action of the Roman Senate or their commanding general. Many during the period of the New Testament came from the aristocratic equestrian (knight) ranks. The Roman army simply did not exist without the effectiveness of this office. Centurions were the most important leaders on the battlefield, the most important messengers, trainers, and even local officials commanding a whole district.

It is only within this context that readers can understand the role of the centurions in the Bible and why events such as the conversion of one of these officers, Cornelius, likely a proto aide-de-camp to Pontius Pilate, was no small matter for either Jew or Gentile. It was a Roman centurion, speculated to be named Longinus, who pierced Jesus's body but then was fully overtaken by the Holy Spirit and recognized Jesus as the son of God. The Roman Catholic Church and several other denominations declare that he converted to Christianity. The office of centurion appears and is pivotal in important events in the books of Matthew, Luke, and Acts. It seems clear that the various and pivotal centurions in the New Testament (Matthew, Mark, Luke, Acts) are historical testimonies to the power of the Holy Spirit.

Ranked below the centurion was the decurion, a junior officer commanding about ten men, most commonly cavalry. Above the centurion was the camp prefect (not to be confused with the prefect of a geographic area like Judea), who was third in command of a legion, an officer who had been a *primus pilus*, or highest-ranking centurion.

Above the centurion and decurion were the senior officers who came from the patrician class. There were two tribune officers, one of who was the second in command of the legion, more often than not the son of a Roman senator and serving in the military as a pathway to the Senate. There were an additional five tribunes who were like staff officers.

The commander of the legion was the legate, some of who were chosen as provincial governors. As mentioned earlier, the equestrian rank also supplied prefects, who held midlevel military and governmental power, and below them, the praetor.

Following the disaster by the former governor of Syria, Varus, in 6 AD, Rome was left with twenty-five legions, around 350,000 troops split between Roman legions and foreign auxiliaries. Their prime job during this second phase of Roman grand strategy was defensively dealing with native revolts (as in the Jewish Great Revolt) or with emerging threats globally.

One question that can often be asked is whether Rome was a violent and cruel state, especially when one looks at events in the Bible. This is especially a concern for modern readers. The answer is simple: Rome was neither more or less violent than its contemporaries. Often, Rome is pictured as the victimizer and the tribes and clients were victims. This is simply not true. The tribes and clients were not only violent with Rome, but they were violent to each other and their own population. In fact, it was the chaos and violence in Judea amongst the Jews with each other that brought Roman intervention in the first place.

Rome did not keep most of its army at home. In fact, the bulk of the Roman army was always abroad. This was done for two reasons. The first reason was military. The enemies of Rome were abroad, and transportation and communication were slow. The second reason was political. Armies that were far from Rome were no immediate threat to the current Roman state.

The Roman army that was located in the lands of the Bible is open to a degree of speculation but is important to understand in the context of the discussion of the Bible and international affairs. Many of the clashes in the biblical lands were not between regular Roman legionnaires and the native population. Judea did not merit the permanent presence of legionnaires for most of the New Testament. Thus, many of the regular Roman soldiers who were not of the equestrian rank or above were most likely auxiliaries or foreign troops that served Rome. Since it was not possible for Jews to serve in the Roman military, if these auxiliaries were from the region, they would have come from the Gentile, likely Greek, population.

Syria became a Roman province in 64 BC under Pompey. It had at any given time three or four Roman legions. In Judea, the seat of Roman power was Caesarea and probably did not have a permanent garrison legion until 70 AD. The original serving legion at the time of Pompey was probably the Third Gallica Legion, who were recruited primarily from Gaul (France). This legion was reformed after the Roman civil war under Caesar and then Mark Antony. During the Jewish revolt of 66 AD, three of its cohorts were wiped out by Jewish insurgents; the remainder of the legion was used in the counteroffensive. The next legion of note is the Fourth Scythian Legion, which was also used in Syria. Both of these legions spent considerable time fighting the Parthians.

The history of the famous Tenth Fretensis Legion is of particular interest to the study of the Bible. Created by Augustus, its members came from Spain, Italy, and Gaul. Records indicate it was stationed in and around Jerusalem in 4 BC and 10 BC, making it likely it was in the region at the time of the birth of Jesus. It was also heavily involved with fighting the Parthians and participated in the ending of the Jewish revolt. The other two legions that may have been in the region were the Sixth Ferrata and the Twelfth Fulminata.

As stated previously, Judea was arguably the most unusual province for the Romans. It never fit well into the Roman international system. Rome attempted to mollify Jewish sensibilities as much as it could while maintaining its vision of order. The Jewish question for the Romans was always seen primarily in the light of international relations. Judea was a critical crossroads and was needed in the bipolar global conflict with Parthia. Yet, many of Rome's problems in Judea were over the clash between the worldviews of Rome and Jerusalem. For example, Pompey had desecrated the Temple in 63 BC and killed or captured support- ers and priests of Aristobulus. In 54 BC, Marcus Crassus, governor of Syria, funded the war against Parthia with Temple funds. In an attempt to gain greater favor with Rome, Herod placed a golden eagle at the Temple entrance, which so enraged the population that it was torn down piece by piece in 4 BC. During Pontius Pilate's prefectship (26–36 BC), he placed images of Caesar on Roman standards in the city, result- ing in a riot, and used money from the Temple to build an aqueduct. Gessius Floris, prefect from 64 to 66 AD, stole money from the Temple, which was probably the spark for the Jewish revolt.

Following Herod's death and the division of Judea, the area became an adjunct to the senatorial province of Syria. The last ethnarch was Herod Archelaus, the son of Herod the Great, but he was removed by Augustus for his incompetence and cruelty to his own people. Thus, the emperor of Rome effectively saved the Jews from one of their own Herodians.

Roman power emanated not from Jerusalem but the Gentile city of Caesarea. Roman prefects who ruled Judea did so from the solace of this mini-Roman capital city, where trips to Jerusalem were made for utilitarian reasons of order and economy. This brings up an important issue: ten cities of the Gospels were Greco-Roman enclaves, including Caesarea, Sepphoris (only four miles from Nazareth), Philadelphia, and Tiberius. The census ordered by Augustus was carried out according to the Bible by Quirinius when he was legate and Coponius was prefect of Judea. This census was done for purposes of taxation and to assess property. Coponius had to crush a Jewish revolt caused by the census. This had been led by Judas of Galilee (often credited with starting the Zealot movement) and Zadok, the priest. They claimed that no taxes should ever be paid to Rome on religious grounds.

One should keep this in mind when looking at Jesus's reaction to the same issue. Normally, a Roman census would also have been done for purposes of military conscription, but this would not have applied to the Jewish population. The Bible tells us that Joseph was afraid of returning to Israel from Egypt because a Herodian was still ruling and therefore was steered to Galilee, where Herod held no power. Modern readers may think of an analogy between the fear of Herod's sons and that of Saddam Hussein or Hafez al-Assad and their sons. The sons of tyrants are often worse than their father. All of this changed once Rome exercised more direct control.

Pontius Pilate

The fifth prefect of Judea (*prefectus iudaeae*) was Pontius Pilate (Matthew, Mark, Luke, John, Acts, and Timothy), who ruled from 26 to 36 AD, accompanied by his "virtuous wife," who some churches have sainted and named Procula. There is evidence that he came from the Ponti family, and others have speculated he may have been born in Franconia (modern Germany). It is also speculated that prior to serving as prefect of Judea, Pilate served in the Roman army in Germania. He may have been a tribune in the Twelfth Legion prior to becoming prefect of Judea, which would have meant he would have been stationed in Syria and been involved in fighting the Parthians. He was of the equestrian rank, and doing well as prefect would have opened doors to greater power in the Roman system. Being an equestrian was insufficient rank to command a legion, and most likely, the troops he commanded were primarily from the region, likely auxiliaries from Caesarea and Sabine, Gentiles of possible Greek origin who had animus for their Jewish neighbors.

Pilate might have had about three thousand soldiers, including one *ala* or cavalry company at his disposal, many of them headquartered in the Antonia Fortress in Jerusalem. There would have been only a few tribunes and centurions of Roman ethnicity. Pilate had asked for regular Roman troops, who he deemed more competent and loyal. Tiberius may have sent him a cohort of Roman citizen volunteers to bolster the defenses at Caesarea.

Pilate's outlook of Judea was very possibly one of frustration and contempt. He likely considered it a land of bandits (*leistai*), insurrectionists, zealots, and assassins (*sicarii*). These criminals and extremists appear in both the Old and New Testament (Genesis, Judges, Kings, Ezra, Jeremiah, Hosea, Matthew, Luke, John, and 2 Corinthians). It is also true that there was incredible synthesis and crossover between all of these categories, with the person being a common bandit one day and an insurrectionist the next.

In a parallel again with the United States, Rome differentiated between those who it went to war with formally and everyone else who were criminals, or criminal combatants. It was said that the disciples and brothers James and John were "sons of thunder" (Mark 3:17) and had revolutionary associations. The sicarii or dagger men were a violent, murderous organization and, in the modern sense, terrorists. It seems highly likely that the most infamous person in the Bible, Judas, with his last name, Iscariot, a derivation of the Latin word *sicarius*, was a sicarii. They were an offshoot of the Zealot movement. In an apt but not perfect analogy, if the Muslim Brotherhood is the larger umbrella movement of Islamic extremists (the Zealots), than ISIS is the most violent offshoot, like the sicarii. The sicarii killed both Romans and Jews, soldiers and civilians. They were noted for raiding the Jewish village of En Gedi and killing over seven hundred civilians. If Judas was sicarii, one could see how betrayed he would have felt by Jesus's failure in his own mind to invite a torrent of violence against Rome.

One has also to remember that this story is quite possible because many Jewish people were victims of bandits and assassins and would have helped Roman troops find them. Jews were not forced into labor for Rome unless they were convicted of a crime. Thus, Roman soldiers served as a rudimentary police force, even if the Romans did it for very utilitarian reasons. It is unclear where the lines between bandit, sicarii, or Zealot were drawn, but to Pilate, all of them would have been his main problem. Barabbas (Matthew, Mark, Luke, John), who the Sanhedrin-inspired crowd traded for Jesus (Matthew, Mark, Acts), was most likely some kind of insurrectionist, whereas those who died on the cross with Jesus were likely bandits (*leistai*). Thus, in modern terms, Rome was engaged in low-intensity warfare and counterinsurgency during its entire time as ruler of Judea during events of the Bible.

Pontius Pilate would have had to navigate through these domestic troubles along with threats and machinations from the world of domestic and international relations emanating from the Sanhedrin as well as Egypt, Syria, and, of course, Parthia.

Pilate, like prefects before and after him, was uninterested in the Jewish religion or Jewish theological debates. Some have suggested that he initially thought he could Romanize the Jews, but this was abandoned. He wanted order, no revolts, and the continued payment of taxes. Something rarely mentioned is that the average term of a prefect of Judea was two years. Pilate was either the longest-serving prefect in history at ten years or a close second. In his first six years, he had no overlord from Syria; for although Lucius Lamia had been appointed legate of Syria, he never stepped foot in the province. This may have led Pilate to be both more independent but also more circumspect, as he had no direct method of appeal.

This is important, as the accepted date of Jesus's crucifixion is 30 AD, which would have been at the time when Pilate had no governor in Syria to confer with, even had he wanted to. It also meant that decisions about Jesus were made at the time when Pilate was in this unique position, rare in Roman times, of having no governor of Syria over him and his extremely long tenure. This situation is quite unique when looking at Roman international relations as a whole. What was in

Pilate's mind knowing that he was one of the most seasoned prefects of his age while having no governor above him? If he had such, would he have sent Jesus to that governor rather than Herod Antipas (Luke 3:19 and Matthew 14:6)?

The trial of Jesus (Mark 15, John 18–19, Matthew 27, Luke 23) must be seen in the context here described. Rome would initially have had no interest in the leader of a Jewish religious group that did not preach violence or revolution. Pilate had to rely on the high priest of Jerusalem for order, whom Rome had appointed. Quirinius had appointed Annas (Luke, Johns, Acts) as high priest when Rome took over in 6 AD. He ruled until 15 AD, when he was deposed by the prefect before Pilate (Gratus), who appointed Annas's son-in-law, Caiaphas, who was high priest when Pilate ruled.

Gratus had changed high priests multiple times until he settled on Caiaphas (Matthew, Luke, John, Acts). Caiaphas was in charge of the Temple treasury, the Jewish Temple police, and the observance of ritual. He had a vested interest in his own position (and that of the other priests) owing his legitimacy to Rome, something rarely mentioned. Jesus's attack against the money lenders posed a direct threat to his class's economic interests. Rome's disinterest in native religious matters that did not threaten its rule was exactly the issue regarding Jesus. Jesus posed no political threat to Rome, so Caiaphas had to lie to Pilate and portray Jesus as a revolutionary. Pilate knew that Emperor Tiberius and his Machiavellian-like stand-in, Sejanus, would be metaphorically watching for signs of disorder. Further, the trial of Jesus came right before or during the downfall of Sejanus. It is quite possible that Tiberius's realization of the treachery of Sejanus, who may have attempted to usurp him, amplified paranoia and suspicion throughout the entire empire. Pilate also knew both to be violent in their wrath. If Jesus claimed to be the political king of the Jews, that would be enough reason for death. When Jesus does not claim such, Pilate saw no threat.

The biblical account paints Pilate in ambiguous terms, some even suggesting he was playing at being Jesus's lawyer. In Matthew 27:14

Pilate "marveled greatly" at Jesus. The Greek in the New Testament uses the word *thaumadzo* which means to be shocked and awed, and be at a loss of words. Pilate disappointed the Sanhedrin by commencing the formalities of a Roman trial rather than merely agreeing with their verdict immediately. Pilate attempted to declare Jesus innocent and, regardless of Procula's failed attempted intervention (Matthew 27:19), buckled under the pressure of the mob. He gave Jesus the standard Roman opportunity to deny charges three times, but Jesus was silent. Further, although many historians question Pilate's attempt to both save Jesus and quell the crowd's passions by offering them the ability to save Jesus or Barabbas, this may have been something he tried precisely because of his unique tenure and more independent position. Jesus was crucified, at the urging of the ruling Jewish class and under the acquiescence of the Roman government. Crucifixion, most associated with Rome, had been used by the Persians, Greeks, Carthaginians, and Jews. However, as a Roman punishment, it became infamous until it became the enduring symbol of the Christian faith, which, like so much in this book, is the story of God's hand in ways that defy human understanding.

Pilate's ordering of the plaque above Jesus reading INRI (Iesus Nazarenus, Rex Iudaeorum), Jesus the Nazarene, King of the Jews (Mark 15:26, Luke 23:38), was less mocking of Jesus and more of an attack against Caiaphas and the Sanhedrin and a demonstration of Pilate's political dominance. Both Tertullian and Eusebius wrote that Pilate reported to Tiberius the story of Jesus's resurrection.

There is considerable controversy about the authenticity of Pilate's letter to Tiberius. The beginning of the letter complains about the province, especially the ruling religious class that Pilate claims is corrupt. The text of the letter indicates that Pilate was impressed with Jesus, felt he was no threat to Rome, and recognized that Jesus could be the son of God. The letter also gives a name, Manilus, to the Roman centurion who spoke the words, "Truly this was the Son of God" (Matthew 27:54). The letter may have been one of the reasons that Tiberius recommended that the Roman Senate make Jesus a god. The Senate rejected this, but it appears that Tiberius held no ill will toward Christians. During this period, Syria finally had a governor in the personage of Lucius Vitellius. At this time, Pilate seemed to have committed multiple errors.

Prior to this, he had to rotate out of Jerusalem one of his cohorts, the Augustana, which bore the image of the emperor on its standards. The Jews of Jerusalem never forgot this attempted abomination. Second, although Pilate had negotiated with Caiaphas to use Temple funds to build a much-needed aqueduct, he was betrayed by the Sanhedrin who, once the project was finished, leaked the funding scheme to a Jerusalem mob led by Zealots and Pilate was forced to take punitive measures to disperse the riot. This allowed the Sanhedrin to have the benefit of the aqueduct and be seen as protector of the faith at the same time. Third, and this may or may not be categorized as a misstep, Pilate removed from the Sanhedrin the right of *jus gladii*, right of the sword. This forbade the Sanhedrin from handing out the death penalty, which would now solely be the jurisdiction only of the Roman authorities. Unwittingly to Pilate, this removed the Sanhedrin's ability to kill Jesus outright, which one could speculate they would have done right after they arrested him to avoid both the displeasure of the people and a killing on Passover when Jesus celebrated the Last Supper.

During Vitellius's governorship, Pilate may have committed an offense against the Jews in Jerusalem by bringing golden shields bearing Tiberius's image into the city and placing them at his palace. The Jews petitioned Tiberius to force Pilate to remove them, possibly being informed on by his enemy, Herod Antipas (New Testament Greek uses the word *ecthra*—hatred—to describe the Pilate/Antipas relationship). Antipas was vying to be the new resurrected king of Judea and viewed Pilate as an obstacle to this. The emperor rebuked Pilate and ordered their removal. This may have marked Pilate for problems. Second, was Pilate's response to a Samaritan leader who claimed to know about treasure buried by Moses at Mount Gerizim. Pilate, perhaps fearing this was a pathway to insurgency, met the rabble before they could reach the destroyed Samaritan temple and killed many and executed the leaders. All of this led Vitellius to recommend that Pilate be removed.

Tiberius recalled Pilate in 36 AD, but Pilate arrived back in Rome after Tiberius died. It is unclear as to why he was recalled—possibly because of Vitellius, but perhaps not. Some have suggested that Caligula, who became emperor in 37 AD, disliked Pilate and ordered him to kill himself, possibly occurring in 38 AD. Other sources suggest Caligula had him executed, and still others claim he converted to Christianity. This was all happening while Herod the Great's grandson, Herod Agrippa, was in Rome. Agrippa had been jailed by Tiberius for insulting the emperor but had made friends with the nephew and adopted son of Tiberius, the infamous Caligula. Whatever Pilate's ultimate fate was, the trial at which he presided was the most important legal trial in history, including its impact on international affairs.

CHAPTER 5

The End of the Beginning

And hath made of one blood all nations of men for to dwell on all the
face of the earth, and hath determined the times before appointed, and
the bounds of their habitation.

—ACTS 17:26

The end of the Bible and international relations historically began with Pilate gone, a new emperor on the throne of Rome, and the coming Great Revolt of the Jews. It was during this period that Christianity takes form as an evangelizing movement among the Gentiles, including and especially among Greek and Roman populations. It was at this time that the Roman citizen Saul the Pharisee becomes St. Paul, and Peter builds the first church. It was the end of the New Testament and the beginning of the faith as a movement.

One of the striking things about this period was the numerous events when Roman officials, often cast as the villain, erupt as the deliverer or as critical to the Christian faith's growth. As previously discussed, the role of the centurion was pivotal to the empire. This should now be understood as surprising considering what these centurions, particularly in Judea, represented. Yet there are seven of them in the New Testament who are important to the belief.

First, was the centurion who trusts Jesus to heal his servant (Luke 7:1–10). This was followed by the centurion who has an epiphany at the crucifixion (Matthew 27:54 and Mark 15:39), named Marius or Manilus by some. The most important was, of course, the conversion of Cornelius (Acts 10:1–7), who was the first named Gentile of the Christian faith. Readers should pause to absorb this. The very first Christian who was not a Jew was none other than a Roman centurion. One can argue that Gentiles can all trace their religious ancestry to Cornelius. Two centurions and one tribune (Claudius Lysias) save Paul from the Jewish mob and from flogging (Acts 22:25–29, Acts 23:23). Lastly is the story and likely conversion of Julius (Acts 27:1–28:16), who saves Paul on his way back to Rome.

With Tiberius dead, perhaps murdered by Caligula, Caligula ruled the empire from 37 to 41 AD and was arguably the worst emperor in Rome's history. His sins and evil actions are too numerous to list and are well known. His crimes were so vast and innumerable that his own Praetorian Guard murdered him and placed Claudius on the throne. One of the critical obsessions that Caligula had for our consideration was that of his own ego and his own "godhood." The result of this was a fanatical program to enforce the emperor's cult, and thus, Judea fell under his gaze.

Relations between Jews and Gentiles in Judea declined further during this period. Herod Agrippa (Acts 25 and 26) engineered the fall of his own uncle, Herod Antipas. When Caligula became emperor, Agrippa, friend to both Caligula and Claudius, regained the title of king of Judea and was the last of the Herodian kings to rule at the sufferance and behest of Rome from 41 to 44 AD. He was seen as a supporter of Judaism and a persecutor of Christianity. A report reached Caligula that a Gentile Greek community had erected an altar to their gods in one of the cities in Judea, which, although done as a provocation by the Greeks, was destroyed by a Jewish mob.

Caligula used this "insult" to establish religious dominance over the Jews, and in 41 AD, ordered his own statue to be erected inside the Temple in Jerusalem. He had ordered the governor (legate) of Syria to enforce this with soldiers. The Jewish crowd said they would rather all be killed than allow this abomination and the legate retreated, not wanting to massacre the people. Caligula ordered the legate's death. However, not only was Caligula murdered soon after this order, but the ship carrying the order was lost.

The throne shifted to Claudius, who ruled from 41 to 54 AD. His rule was engineered not only by the Pretorian Guard but also with the help at some level of his friend Herod Agrippa, who was already rewarded for his close ties with and sponsorship of the Julio-Claudians. Claudius practiced religious toleration, reversing Caligula's obsession, and expanded the empire to include Britain. He was murdered by his wife, Agrippina, so that her son, Nero (2 Timothy 4:22), could assume the throne.

Nero, the last of the Julio-Claudians, was perhaps the second-worst emperor in Rome's history. He ruled until 68 AD, when he was either murdered or committed suicide. His evils, like Caligula's, were too numerous to count. The allegation that he was responsible for the great fire of 64 AD, which he blamed on the Christians, and that he then used it to amplify the persecution of the Christians is essential in discussing the events at the end of the New Testament. Nero, the most anti-Christian emperor to date, was the exact emperor at the time of Peter and Paul's great mission and proves the irony that his empire would eventually become the greatest proselytizer for the faith by the time we reach Constantine.

The Roman government on the ground in Syria/Judea during this later period of the New Testament was in turmoil. Its actions led directly to the Great Revolt and the end of the Temple. Many of these prefects following Pilate were of low quality. Perhaps an analogy that will appeal to historians is that of the second sons of nobility during the medieval era, especially as it relates to this region of the world. Second sons were often packed off to the Crusades, as they had no prospects at home, yet were still "aristocrats." The quality was assuredly mixed.

The prefect following Pilate, Cuspius Fadus, only lasted two years. A false prophet by the name of Theudas (Acts 5:36) instigated a revolt and led thousands to the Jordan River, where Fadus attacked them and killed over four hundred people. Ventidius Cumanus, prefect of Judea from 48 to 52 AD, and Marcus Antonius Felix, from 52 to 58 AD, were noted for cruelty. Cumanus increased tensions between Rome and the Jews, and he further amplified the conflict between Jews and Samaritans, siding with the Samaritans (who had probably bribed him). This led to legate of Syria Quadratus's intervention and his execution of many Jews and Samaritans in order to quell the violence between both. He also executed some of the auxiliary forces from Sebaste and Caesarea, who had used the period to exact greater violence on the Jewish population. Felix (Acts 23, 24, 25) was noted, even by the Roman historian Tacitus, for doing "any evil act with impunity" along with his fellow prefect.

Saul, who became Paul, was from Tarsus, known as a university city at the time. His conversion to Christianity on the road to Damascus (Acts 9:3–9) is an interesting case study of this period, especially from the international relations perspective. A student of Gamaliel the Elder (Acts 5:34 and 22:3), Saul was a Roman citizen (Acts 21:39), and there are debates as to why. One strong theory is that a near ancestor had done particular service to Rome, and thus Saul was a legacy; another was that Julius Caesar had granted the people of Tarsus Roman citizenship.

Regardless of the reason, Saul was a Roman citizen, and this creates an entirely new experience and understanding viewing his treatment as Paul and his evangelizing to the Gentiles. Paul, as is often stated by serious theologians, is the second or third most crucial figure in Christianity following Jesus and Peter. Paul was likely born in 5 AD to a devoutly religious family and studied to become a Pharisee. He was highly educated and is often characterized as a religious Jew yet highly Hellenized.

In so many ways, Paul, as a person and as a saint, is the culmination of this entire book from the earthly perspective as Jesus is the culmination of this book from a universal standpoint. Paul's Hellenized education was made possible by the machinations of the Greek and Persian empires. His Roman citizenship due to the rise of the Roman Republic in the Mediterranean and his birth and education through the period of the early imperial era are all a result of the tectonic shifts in international relations that have occurred thus far. His familiarity with Greco-Roman culture, philosophy, and religion allowed him to seamlessly engage with the Gentile communities of the Roman Empire like no other apostle. Nine of the Pauline epistles are addressed to Gentile churches. Further were his choice of locations for evangelizing, such as where he preached in Athens, around 51 AD—a good example is the famous Agora, from where he was led to the Areopagus.

Paul's arrests are dealt with differently because of his Roman citizenship. This came to the forefront bluntly when he was bound and threatened with flogging. It may not seem as a big deal to modern readers, but a quote from Cicero's Verrine Orations may lend perspective: "To bind a Roman citizen is a crime, to flog an abomination, and to slay him is almost an act of murder." It may interest American readers that Cicero dominated the thinking of many of the American founders, including Hamilton, Adams, and Washington. This makes the story of Paul so mesmerizing.

In 51 AD, Paul was preaching in Philippi and cast out a demon who had possessed a "fortune teller slave girl" (Acts 16:16–40). The casting out of the demon enraged the owner of the girl because she'd lost her "fortune telling" ability. The owner complained to the Roman authorities. Paul was brought before the Roman magistrate, who ordered him to be flogged the next day. An earthquake resulted in Paul going free, whereby he demanded an apology of the Roman officials because he was a Roman citizen. Paul was released, in part because the officials feared that their actions against a Roman citizen could lose the privileged status that the city of Philippi enjoyed under the empire.

In 57 AD, Paul reentered Jerusalem, where he rejoined James, the brother of Jesus. James convinced Paul that he should demonstrate to the Jews and new Christians that he still respected the Torah, and

Paul attempted to engage in purification rituals at the Temple. At this point, a Jewish mob arrived and claimed that Paul was trying to defile the Temple (Acts 21:28). They began to beat him to death. The Romans (Acts 22–23) stopped the riot and took Paul away in chains. Paul informed them he was a Roman citizen. He attempted to quiet the crowd protected by the Romans, which resulted in further consternation and the Roman commander ordering him to be flogged. This was stopped by the Roman centurion, reminding the commander that Paul was a Roman citizen.

The next day, Paul was led to the Sanhedrin. This went poorly, as the corrupt high priest Ananias was obsessed with killing Paul and wanted him executed like Jesus. He tried to convince the Romans that Paul was guilty of sedition, but it backfired on two fronts. In the supernatural realm, Jesus came to Paul that night and told him to evangelize in Rome, the legacy of which cannot be measured (Acts 23:11). In the earthly realm, the Roman commander, a tribune, Claudius Lysias, ordered an escort of two hundred Roman soldiers (a significant force) to protectively move him to Caesarea to face the prefect, Felix. Felix toyed with Paul for two years under arrest and attempted to ransom him (Acts 24:24–27). In 59 AD, the procurator (Romans changed title from prefect) of Judea, Porcius Festus (Acts 25), attempted to convince Paul to return to Jerusalem to be tried. Paul knew what awaited him there and did the one thing that only a Roman citizen could do and thus obey Jesus's commandment: he declared he had a right as a Roman citizen to appeal to Caesar. Paul was unwilling to be tried by a mere provincial court when the emperor could try him. Thus, the famous passage in the book of Acts (25:10–12):

> Then said Paul, "I stand at Caesar's judgment seat, where I ought to be judged. To the Jews I have done no wrong, as you very well know. For if I am an offender, or have committed anything deserving of death, I do not object to dying; but if there is nothing in these things of which these men accuse me, no one

can deliver me to them. I appeal to Caesar." Then Festus, when he had conferred with the council, answered, "You have appealed to Caesar? To Caesar, you shall go!"

Festus was desperate to calm things down with the Jews in Judea and was willing to use Paul as that tool.

Festus attempted to rope Agrippa into the conflict, but Agrippa believed Paul should be freed. However, Paul had appealed to Caesar and left for Rome by sea. During the voyage, Paul's ship was shipwrecked. The Roman soldiers wished to kill the prisoners for expediency, but they were stopped by the Roman centurion in charge, Julius, who had come to respect and admire Paul, fulfilling God's prophecy. Paul spent at least two years under house arrest in Rome waiting for his trial. It was believed Nero had him beheaded, a Roman citizen, around 64 AD.

The Great Revolt: The End of Judea in International Relations

The Great Revolt, often referred to as the First Jewish-Roman War, began in 66 AD. It did not end until 73 AD. The revolt erupted during the tumultuous reign of Emperor Nero and under the Roman governor (legate) of Syria, Cestius Gallus, and the Roman prefect of Judea, Gessius Florus.

Florus, according to Tacitus, was incompetent by Roman standards. He had been appointed to his position by Nero, whose wife was a friend of Florus's wife. He had a consistent hatred against the Jews and favored the Greek population. After a Greek group defiled a synagogue, Florus took money from the Jewish community to hear the case and then imprisoned the Jewish petitioners. Additionally, he stole money from the Temple treasury. This last criminal act was the spark that started the bonfire, creating violent riots.

Florus responded to the protests about his thievery by imprisoning many of the Jewish leaders. This led to a massive uprising that overran the Roman garrison. The surviving Roman soldiers were promised parole if they surrendered, but in an act that would reverberate throughout Rome, they laid down their arms and were murdered. Florus and Herod Agrippa fled.

Massacres of Gentiles by Jews broke out in places like Decapolis and Ascalon, and of Jews by Gentiles in places like Caesarea. This violence began to spread throughout the empire in cities like Antioch and Alexandria. Cestius Gallus, legate of Syria, fearing it would turn into a full-blown rebellion, took the Twelfth Fulminata Legion, with elements from other legions, along with the Jewish forces of Agrippa to crush the rebels. Cestius, like Varus in Germania, was full of bravado, overconfidence, and contempt for the Jewish insurgents. Not only was the legion ambushed, losing at least five thousand men, but its eagle was taken, the ultimate humiliation for Rome.

While a Jewish government was formed, Rome dispatched General Vespasian and his son Titus to deal with the rebels with four legions. Factional fighting between the various Jewish groups—Zealots, Pharisees, Sadducees, and sicarii—broke out, leading to atrocity and counter-atrocity. While the Roman army was outside the gates of Jerusalem, the Zealots and sicarii murdered at least twenty thousand fellow Jews. The death of Nero happened during this time, which created political turmoil in Rome and ultimately led Vespasian (following the fighting between Galba, Otho, and Vitellius) to become emperor of Rome, leaving Titus in command. Titus besieged Jerusalem and attempted peace talks, offering terms that allowed the Jews to continue practicing their faith with their Temple if they threw down their arms, but he was refused. The city finally fell in 71 AD, fulfilling the prophecy made about Jerusalem by Jesus:

> For the days shall come upon thee, that thine enemies shall cast a trench about thee, and compass thee round, and keep thee in on every side, And shall lay thee even with the ground, and thy children within thee; and they shall not leave in thee one stone

upon another; because thou knewest not the time of thy visitation. (Luke 19:43–44)

The end of the revolt concluded with the destruction of the Temple (John 4:20–24, Matthew 23:37–24:2, Mark 13:1–2, Luke 13:34–35, Luke 21:5–6, 20), the nullification of the Sadducees, the diaspora of the Jewish people, and the destruction of a Jewish homeland until the re-creation of Israel in 1948.

CHAPTER 6

Trade and Commerce
in the Bible

Then he that had received the five talents went and traded
with the same, and made them other five talents.

—MATTHEW 25:16

Trade and commerce are a significant part of international relations, though it often takes a back seat to what is termed in modern IR language "hard-power" threats to national security. One of the many myths surrounding modern international relations is that we live in an age of globalization. In actuality, globalization has usually been the rule rather than the exception, and the periods of the Bible represent this. Just as today, trade and resources, or lack thereof, motivated the geopolitics of nations. Just as historical Japan's lack of resources in the early twentieth century led to an attempt at expansion and the resultant Second World War, so for example did the Assyrian lack of resources motivate its attempts at expansion and empire. This economic competition was no different for the Egyptians, Babylonians, Persians, Greeks, Parthians, or Romans.

Trade is mentioned in Genesis, Ezekiel, Matthew, and Revelation. During Abraham's time, there was a vibrant trade route via caravan from Palmyra to Damascus, to Galilee, and on to Phoenician ports.

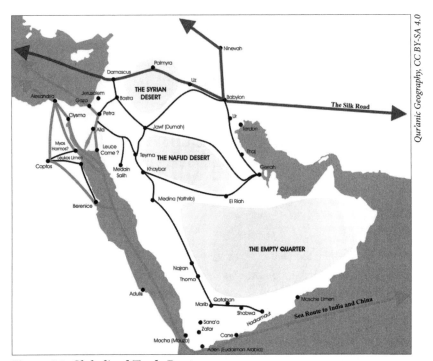

Figure 6-1: Globalized Trade Routes

This route mirrored much of Abraham's travels, where he left a prosperous area to do God's will. During this time, Canaan was a link between Egypt and Asia, and this would continue until its apex during Roman rule.

In the Old Testament, there was the Via Maris (the Way of the Sea, Isaiah 9:1 and Matthew 4:15), the Trunk Road, and the Coastal Road channeling travel and trade between Galilee, Samaria, and Damascus. There was the King's Highway (Isaiah 19:23), which connected ancient Egypt to Somaliland, Aqaba, and on to Damascus and the Euphrates River valley. The Romans later paved these roads.

Plantation farming was hugely important to Egypt, where they grew corn, wheat, and fruits. Egypt had caravan and sea routes that linked it to Mesopotamia, Asia Minor, and the Persian Gulf. Records indicate

Figure 6-2: Paul's First Missionary Journey

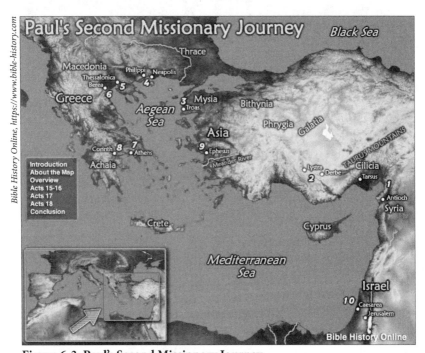

Figure 6-3: Paul's Second Missionary Journey

Figure 6-4: Paul's Third Missionary Journey

trade of the time involved copper and linen from Egypt, gold and ivory from Somaliland, silver from Anatolia, purple dyes from Canaan, vases from Crete, and spice and incense from Arabia. They used a measuring system that frequently appears in the Bible, the cubit, which was a measurement from the bottom of the elbow to the end of a person's middle finger, roughly eighteen inches. Goliath (1 Samuel 17:4) was six cubits, or over nine feet tall.

The Persian Empire utilized a system of interconnected roads and caravans that linked to Phoenician and Greek ships. Persia standardized measures, lengths, and a monetary system. It had an elaborate tribute and tax system and heavily used the Way of the Sea and the King's Highway. It also standardized the omnipresent biblical measurement of the cubit (Genesis, Exodus, Numbers, Deuteronomy, Joshua,

Judges, Samuel, Kings, Chronicles, Ezra, Nehemiah, Esther, Jeremiah, Ezekiel, Daniel, Zechariah, Matthew, Luke, John, and Revelation).

Long-distance trade in and around the Mediterranean has existed since at least the Bronze age (3000 to 1200 BC) and was exponentially amplified by Greco-Roman empires. In Ezekiel 27, we see that Tarshish, which most consider to be ancient Tyre (Joshua, Samuel, Kings, Chronicles, Ezra, Psalms, Isiah, Joel, Matthew, Mark, Luke, and Acts), traded vastly with Israel and the world. We know the Tyrians traded throughout the Mediterranean all the way to Spain. Solomon's wealth came through trade and a maritime alliance with Hiram, king of Tyre, and the Queen of Sheba.

During King Solomon's time, there were a plethora of trade routes between Asia Minor, Syria, and Egypt. The hub of these routes was Solomon's kingdom. His wealth was vast and amazing (Kings 10:14–29, 2 Chronicles 2:17–18; 8:7–10). The overland caravan route to Sheba terminated in Solomon's Israel. Solomon had a fantastic trading fleet that traded in ivory, sandalwood, animals, copper, silver, and gold. These last three were part of the famous legend about King Solomon's mines. These may have been located in the Timna Valley in southern Israel and the Jordan Rift Valley. During the Jews' trials and tribulations under the heel of the Babylonians and Persians, the Judean Jews maintained links to the Jews under captivity. These contacts continued for centuries afterward.

One of the most unfortunate fuels to the economy of the entire Bible was the slave trade. Slavery is a major theme of the Bible, especially against the Jewish people. The Egyptians pressed Jews into forced labor as slaves, the Babylonians forced them into harsh captivity, and the Persians detained them until eventually liberating them. The Roman economy was based on slaves performing labor in cities and on farms. Notably, slaves in the ancient world, especially Athens and later Rome, often occupied higher positions than non-slaves, such as the Greek tutors who were slaves to important Roman families. Manumission in Rome was also common where freemen could serve in prominent positions such as a ship's captain or administrator. It is speculated that Felix, the incompetent governor of Judea, was a Greek freedman.

Money and monetary issues appear over the entirety of the Bible. As is true today, money was a tool of political and international relations power as coins illustrated rulers, such as Caesar's image on the coin Jesus is confronted with. Approximate modern values of the currency range widely, and in some ways it is a fool's errand to give modern calculations. Just like converting foreign currency today into dollars gives you a false picture, so do attempts to do so for antiquity unless one looks at the purchasing power parity (PPP), which tells what could be exchanged in that economy for a certain amount. Economies that are based on precious metals have high purchasing rates for small amounts unless that same currency unit is debased by inferior metals. This became a problem for the later Roman Empire, as an example. A mite was 1/8 cent, a drachma was 16 cents, a half shekel was 32 cents, a shekel was 64 cents, and a pound of silver was about $20. A pound of gold was between $300 and $600, and a talent of silver $1,000. Finally, a talent of gold was $20,000 to $40,000. If we put this in an Old Testament perspective, Solomon has an annual revenue of 666 (the number of the Beast in Revelation) talents of gold (1 Kings 10–14). Using this calculation, Solomon's personal wealth, not counting innumerable property, would have been around $26 million a year. If property is added, some scholars claim he may have been a trillionaire in wealth.

During the Roman period, the denari was worth about $2 to $4, which would be a day's laborers wage, and one could use a PPP value of x10, perhaps more. A sesterce would be about 50 cents to $1, and an aureus (gold coin) was close to $20. A bottle of olive oil would cost perhaps $5 and a loaf of bread about $2. A Roman senator, who did not draw a public salary, might have an income of 1,200,000 sestertii (roughly equal to dollars), an equestrian like Pilate 400,000, and a Roman legion soldier 1,200. Gold as metal would hardly ever be touched by a commoner, and a talent, only in their wildest dreams. These figures should enlighten the reader when one looks at the parable of the talents, as these were, literally, kingly sums.

Globalization of the Greeks

Greek globalization was vast and dominated the Mediterranean. Unlike the Roman experience, it was a globalization of linked city-states. Thus, instead of creating a globalized empire, it created a Hellenized empire. Greek globalization spread Greek culture, art, language, products, and ideas. This was part and parcel of the clash previously mentioned in Judea. This globalization of the material and intellectual property of Greece set the stage for the Roman experience and the Gentile settlements in the Middle East.

Rome and Globalization

It is clear the most significant impact of globalization during the New Testament biblical period was thanks to Rome. Rome's globalization spread Roman influence, Roman law, Roman values, and Roman

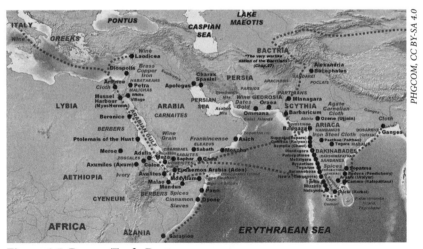

Figure 6-5: Roman Trade Routes

civilization. Latin was the *lingua franca* of the empire and of trade, exactly how English is today. The Roman international trade system stretched from ports like Berenice on the Red Sea and Mykonos in the Mediterranean, and it allowed Rome to trade with India, Sri Lanka, and Han dynasty China. The first recognizable Silk Road, long before Marco Polo, stretched from China to the Mediterranean by the first century BC. From North Africa and Asia, Rome bought silk, cotton, gems, pearls, scents, and pepper. It bought wheat from Egypt, olive oil from Spain, and wine from France. During the time of the New Testament, Rome purchased so much of these goods that there was a massive imbalance of trade and payments, which should sound very familiar to modern readers.

Like the modern age, Roman citizens enjoyed a high standard of living by exploiting the wealth of their provinces, clients, and trading partners. Roman globalization created a culture of affluence, one of bathhouses and temple building. Two Roman constructions provide concrete examples of wealth for both ideological and economic reasons. The first were Rome's famous roads. During the time of Jesus, Rome had built fifty thousand miles of road with milestone markers bearing Rome's insignia as a sign of political and military dominance worldwide. Famous roads like the Appian Way (350 miles from Rome to Brindisi), the Via Flaminia (200 miles from Rome to the Adriatic), Via Egnatia (300 miles from the Adriatic to the Aegean to Turkey), and the Britain Fosse Way (230 miles from Cornwall to northeast England) are still in use today. These roads were about twenty feet in width and had a slight rise in the middle to drain water (an idea still used today). They were dotted with postal houses and inns and protected by the Roman army. They were also lined with government residences. A legion could travel on such roads at twenty miles a day. In fact, our word "mile" comes from the Latin *mille*, or one thousand strides, which equaled five thousand feet, which was how Rome measured the travel of a Roman soldier. Many argue that travel would not be as good until the emergence of the railroad. It was on these very roads that Paul evangelized the Gentile population. The second form of construction was the Roman aqueducts. Hundreds were built throughout the empire for both utilitarian and political presence purposes. As previously noted, the construction of the one in Jerusalem caused great consternation. These were constructed primarily from the fourth century B.C. to the third century A.D. The Roman capital had about eleven aqueduct systems alone, and like the Roman roads, some are still in use today, such as the one that supplies the Trevi Fountain.

Trade was primarily carried out by the private sector—merchants, *mercatores*, who often had state contracts and created the flow of goods. Roman merchants preceded the legions, such as in Gaul, or otherwise followed army units while they traveled and camped. The Roman private sector also included bankers and businessmen, *negotatores*, along with farmers and ranchers.

Most infamous in the Bible were the publicans, who served *publicani* or tax-collecting companies. The publicans in the Bible (mentioned in both Matthew and Luke) were often loathed by Roman and foreigner alike. Many were corrupt, engaging in fraud and overcharging their constituents. They would then pocket the extra that Rome did not require, often creating enormous problems for the local Roman government in places like Judea. Many viewed them as corrupt and traitors to their own people. This should put in clear perspective the attitude that Jesus had about eating and commiserating with the publicans (the Pharisees even criticized Jesus for this), as well as the amplified astonishment toward the disciple Matthew, who was a publican. The publicans received huge profits because of the insatiable demand the Romans had for consumer goods.

This Roman globalization led to Roman excursions and settlements in India, Sri Lanka, China, and the Baltic. Rome fought wars for natural resources in places like Garamantes (North Africa), where it wanted gold, salt, and wild animals. One of the fascinating aspects of this period is to study the level of industrialization (often done by studying archaeological pollution deposits). Once Rome fell (476 AD), the level of industrialization at the time of Jesus would not again be as high until the industrial revolution of the eighteenth and nineteenth centuries. This gives us a fantastic window into the level of economic activity during the time of the New Testament.

Judea for Rome was a crossroads, and the coastal road through Judea led to the breadbasket of the empire, Egypt. Roman military settlements created stability, better trade routes, and markets. Judea was integrated into the Roman system of globalization as a Roman province. Domestically, it relied on the influx of pilgrims and offerings to the Temple, though it had limited resources save for fish, balsam, and asphalt.

The Roman navy kept the sea lanes open. Critical to the global system of that age, and similar to its importance from the nineteenth century to today, was Rome's anti-piracy efforts, such as Pompey the Great's campaign of 60 BC, which allowed Rome to extend onward into the Holy Land. Rome's merchant marine was larger than any other European state's until the eighteenth century, and a merchant could safely get his goods from the Bay of Naples to the port of Alexandria in about two weeks. This naval stability only occurs two other times in the history of international relations: during the height of the Pax Britannica, from the nineteenth to early twentieth century, and the Pax Americana today.

Rome's dominance of the Mediterranean meant Roman protection for merchants, which led to ease of transport and safe routes that would eventually take the disciples of Jesus across the waters and ultimately to Rome. Indeed, Roman transportation and ingenuity sped up its eventual conversion to Christianity. In the end, Roman earthly economic power created the conditions for God to spread his faith to all of Europe and beyond.

CHAPTER 7

Freedom, Liberty, and the Legacy of Jesus

And seeing the multitudes, he went up into a mountain: and when he
was set, his disciples came unto him:
And he opened his mouth, and taught them, saying,
Blessed are the poor in spirit: for theirs is the kingdom of heaven.
Blessed are they that mourn: for they shall be comforted.
Blessed are the meek: for they shall inherit the earth.
Blessed are they which do hunger and thirst after righteousness:
for they shall be filled.
Blessed are the merciful: for they shall obtain mercy.
Blessed are the pure in heart: for they shall see God.
Blessed are the peacemakers: for they shall be called
the children of God.
Blessed are they which are persecuted for righteousness sake:
for theirs is the kingdom of heaven.
Blessed are ye, when men shall revile you, and persecute you,
and shall say all manner of evil against you falsely, for my sake.

—MATTHEW 5:1–11

How does one write about the legacy of life? C. S. Lewis said that he could never write a heavenly version of *The Screwtape Letters* (an allegorical Christian apologetic tale dedicated to J. R. R. Tolkien,

115

based on the correspondence between a major and minor devil) since it would be impossible for a human to truly illustrate God's design. In essence, this is the problem with writing about the legacy of Jesus, in this case, to international relations.

Jesus changes every aspect of every field of human endeavor. In the often dry-toast world of international relations, we forget this. I am reminded of an experience I had addressing an audience at the graduate school of International World Politics in Washington, DC. I had just finished a lengthy presentation on the grand strategy of the United States, and I was taking questions. I was expounding on the need for an American Doctrine foundationally based on the natural law of God, which in the modern age would require nations to uphold democratic values and intervene against tyranny, genocide, and persecution. A questioner in the audience asked how I could possibly justify this. I looked perhaps as incredulous as her and said, "I am a Christian."

Jesus injects into the stale world of international affairs the admonition and the promise of justice, mercy, and love. Jesus's teachings form the core of morality in international affairs and therefore to classical liberalism's promise of freedom and justice, and crusading realism's promise of protection and truth. Enlightenment Christian thinkers like John Locke, the most pivotal thinker to the American Founding Fathers, translated this into natural law, seen in the Declaration of Independence as "the Laws of Nature and of Nature's God" and in *Two Treatises of Government* as "life, health, liberty, or possessions," changed in the Declaration to "Life, Liberty, and the pursuit of Happiness." This happiness is the happiness of eudemonia (not euphoria), meaning living a life of virtue. It is in essence the modern Christian life and dictates the Christian's actions in foreign affairs.

On the other side are many experts who deny even Jesus's existence. They make up a sizeable percentage of academics worldwide. Many of these same people would be comfortable relying on non-biblical sources for their history. Yet even Flavius Josephus, writing in the crown jewel of non-biblical Jewish history about this era, stated in 93 AD:

> About this time there lived Jesus, a wise man, if indeed one ought to call him a man. For he was one who performed surprising deeds and was a teacher of such people as accept the truth gladly. He won over many Jews and many of the Greeks. He was the Messiah... He appeared to them spending a third day restored to life, for the prophets of God had foretold these things and a thousand other marvels about him. And the tribe of the Christians, so called after him, has still to this day not disappeared.

The Jewish Talmud severely criticizes Jesus, who, if having never existed, would not be worthy of any mention. Six Greco-Roman authors mention Jesus and often Pilate as well as the rise of Christianity: Tacitus, Suetonius, Serapion, Pliny the Younger, Clement of Rome, and Ignatius of Antioch. Mara bar Serapion's letter is very intriguing, as it mentions the idea of the new law being established. This new law is the new covenant with God through Jesus.

The greatest impact regarding international relations and politics in general is the biblical discussion of the state. Recall Jesus's famous altercation with the Pharisees when he replies, "Then saith he unto them, render therefore unto Caesar the things which are Caesar's; and unto God the things that are God's" (Matthew 22:21). Jesus consistently rebuked the political ruling class of Judea, the Pharisees and Sadducees, for their hypocrisy and corruption. This is known as the eight woes mentioned in Matthew 23:

> They taught about God but did not love God; they devoured widows houses; they preached about God, but converted people to a dead religion; they taught that an oath sworn by the temple or altar was not binding; they taught the Law but did not practice it; they presented a surface appearance of being clean; they exhibited themselves as righteous, but were not; and they professed a high

regard for the dead prophets, but they were the ones who persecuted and murdered.

This is further exemplified by Jesus's cleansing of the Temple of the
money changers and merchants (Matthew 12:12–17, Mark 11:15–19, John
2:13–16, and Luke 19:45–48).

For the Jews, the legacy of the Bible in international relations is
mixed. The Jewish meta-narrative during this biblical period went
through three phases. The first was that of the tradition of Moses, where
Moses led the people from Egypt in the Exodus, was forced to wander
in the wilderness, but was promised the land of Israel. The second
phase was that of Zion (2 Samuel 5:7), leading to the tradition of kingship (Saul, David, Solomon) and the central role of the Temple. The last
biblical phase was that of captivity and oppression, culminating in the
dispersion.

This final legacy created the Jewish diaspora, which was a result of
the Jewish revolt ending in the destruction of the Temple in 70 AD, not
only leading to the destruction of much of Jerusalem but also to the
Romans renaming the city Aelia Capitolina, placing a Roman colony
there, banning Jews from the city, and building a temple to Jupiter
where the Temple of Solomon once stood. This solidified with the Bar
Kokhba revolt between 132 and 136 AD, which led to a complete and
final diaspora. Thus the international politics of the day played its role
in creating a new Jewish identity and tradition that was not dependent
on the Temple for it to survive.

Yet the story of the Jews, the Bible, and international relations comes
full circle with the advent of Zionism, which was the most powerful
movement for the Jews in international relations in the modern age
and traces a direct ancestral line to the Old Testament. In fact, it is the
entire justification for the modern state of Israel founded in 1948. As a
result of the international politics of Europe in the nineteenth century,
warfare and territorial acquisition in central and eastern Europe, and
oppressive discrimination in places like Britain and France, Zionism as

a movement was born. Zionism's basic goal was for the Jewish people to reclaim their God-given rights over Israel, and so the international politics and actions from the Kingdom of Ur through the Roman Empire set the stage for the Israel we know today.

For Rome, the very government that oppressed the Jews and crucified Jesus began to crack as the conversions of Cornelius, Lysius, Julius, and others took over the very empire that persecuted Christians. And then, in an act that can only be attributed to God, that very empire ensured the triumph of Christianity in Western civilization and beyond.

The Christian legacy is beyond calculation, but it also ushered in the great Christian dilemma in politics and international relations. Modern theologians like Reinhold Niebuhr attempted to have it both ways in the creation of Christian realism. It recognizes the sinfulness of man and his freedom of action. Niebuhr rightly condemns the trend among progressives to claim that humanity can be perfect and rightly rejects the progressive's blind faith in progress. It validates the Great Commandment (first two of the Ten Commandments) but emphasizes that states will act in their own interest. It condemns the idea of creating a Kingdom of Heaven on earth, or even attempting it. Christian realism seems in line with the Bible in its recognition of the fallen humanity, but it also seems to hand off responsibility for the evil done to others or to no one. It is both Christian and realist, but it does not offer a biblical solution to how Christians should follow the Bible and engage in international relations.

On the one hand, there is Romans 13: "Let every soul be subject unto the higher powers. For there is no power but of God: the powers that be are ordained of God." On the other hand, is Acts 5:29: "We ought to obey God rather than men." Luke 4:18–19 states: "The Spirit of the Lord is upon me, because he hath anointed me to preach the gospel to the poor; he hath sent me to heal the brokenhearted, to preach deliverance to the captives, and recovering of sight to the blind, to set at liberty them that are bruised."

The entire dilemma is encapsulated in Matthew 22:21: "Render therefore unto Caesar the things which are Caesar's; and unto God the things that are God's." Just as the Second Amendment in the Bill of Rights is not read in its entirety, partisans of either side do the same with Jesus. Jesus clearly states one should give to the government what belongs or pertains to the government, but he also tells us that you must give God what is His. Jesus's attacks on the ruling class of Judea for hypocrisy and corruption is this idea made flesh. For those advocating natural law in international affairs (or politics in general), perhaps most important to heed is Romans 2:15: "Which shew the work of the law written in their hearts, their conscience also bearing witness, and their thoughts the mean while accusing or else excusing one another." (This is also expressed in the Old Testament in Hebrews 8:10.)

The law written on our hearts is the law God has imprinted on humanity, individually and universally. This is expressed by St. Jerome and St. Thomas as synderesis, the innate knowledge of morality coming from God. Natural law Christian theologians using Aristotelian methods to prescribe human action in this area boiled it down to "doing good, and avoiding evil." The idea of *civitas* (political society) emerges from this synderesis, and citizenship means putting the common good before private gain. Evil and corrupt regimes stifle this, and therefore stifle God and prevent us from rendering to God what is God's. Therefore, an evil regime or an evil law must be disobeyed for one to be right with God.

St. Augustine attempted to bridge the gap by illustrating the City of Man and the City of God. He maintained that states need to maintain order, and citizens must obey their laws. However, rulers cannot establish any law and expect obedience if that law contradicts God's will. Obedience to God comes first. War in international relations, Augustine asserts, is a necessity due to the fall of humanity, and he created a rudimentary rule of warfare when he stated that Christian soldiers should go to war mournfully and take not delight in killing.

Augustine's attempt continues to amplify the Christian dilemma in international affairs.

The biblical impact on international relations continues. Five pillars of Christian tradition create the modern moral landscape of international affairs. These are the Law of Nations (*Jus Gentium*), the Truce of God (*Treuga Dei*), the Peace of God (*Pax Dei*), Just War (*Jus ad Bellum*), and Justice in War (*Jus in Bello*). These human laws strive for peace, order, safety, and virtue. There can be no Geneva Conventions, ban against biological weapons, or abhorrence of genocide without this biblical tradition. The Law of Nations originally created by the Romans to govern the proper conduct of international affairs is Christianized by creating the most powerful argument and type of international law called the Naturalist School, where laws and customs between nations are based on international law; but that law derives from natural principles guided by divine direction. A nation does not sink a passenger ship on the high seas during war, as one of thousands of examples. During the early medieval period, the Peace of God was an attempt by the Church to put fences around people and places during warfare to protect priests, monks, nuns, farmers and farms, and church property. Related to this was the Truce of God attempting to limit the days and times that warfare could occur.

Largely attributed to St. Thomas Aquinas, during the middle of the Middle Ages he codified the concepts of "just war" and "justice in war." These were originally Greco-Roman concepts, but again, they were made Christian and biblical to reflect the impact of Jesus. It is the standard today in the twenty-first century of how states should go to war, what they can and cannot due. It is the Bible in action in its starkest legacy to contemporary international affairs. It is the entire justification of events such as the Nuremberg and Tokyo war crimes trials, the UN Charter on Human Rights, and the heart and soul of American foreign policy.

Just war recognizes the evil of warfare, but also of man's fall (as did St. Augustine). If war must happen, it must be minimal and as just as possible. War can only be fought to defend people and defend justice. War can be engaged for self-defense and to protect the innocent, defend allies, reclaim what was stolen, restore peace, or obey God's command. Justice in war requires states to only attack combatants; civilians cannot be deliberately targeted. The war must be in good faith, and proportional. The negative aspects of the war cannot be greater than its moral justification. War cannot rely on immoral means to achieve its ends, such as torture, and combatants who surrender or who are wounded must be protected and tended to. This was why the world was horrified by Nazi, Soviet, and Japanese atrocities during the Second World War and the genocide conducted by the various communist states of the twentieth and twenty-first century. It is why people trying to be good are repulsed by the actions of North Korea, China, Syria, and Iran in the twenty-first century.

The end of the New Testament prior to Revelations is Paul's evangelizing of the Gentiles and his use of his own Hellenized education, which began to engulf the Western world even before his death. Paul used Jesus's teachings to educate the world on Christian liberty (Leviticus 25:10, Isaiah 61:1, Jeremiah 34:8–17, Luke 4:18, Romans 8:21, 2 Corinthians 3:17, Galatians 2:4 and 5:1, James 2:12), freeing mankind from the bondage of sin through the blood of Jesus and the constraints of Jewish law. John 8:36 is particularly powerful: "If the Son therefore shall make you free, ye shall be free indeed." Jesus creates a standard of perfect righteousness and justice that no earthly kingdom can attain but all can strive for. Christianity builds on Greco-Roman concepts of *jus naturale*, natural law, a law that follows divine intent to give it true form for the first time through the Holy Trinity. As the American Revolution is the second most important event in world history, it is no coincidence that it is directly dependent on the utmost important event of world history, the resurrection of Jesus Christ and his teaching. American readers should focus intently on this. The entire legitimacy of the founding of the United States is based upon natural law, which is only made flesh in the birth and life of Jesus.

In the year 1630, sailing from Yarmouth, England, to the New World, Jonathan Winthrop gave his famous sermon that has been memorialized in countless passages in American history:

> For we must consider that we shall be as a city upon a hill. The eyes of all people are upon us. So that if we shall deal falsely with our God in this work we have undertaken, and so cause him to withdraw his present help from us, we shall be made a story and a byword throughout the world.

In other words, the first Americans believed that removing God from their daily lives would render any future impossible, thus reducing them to a footnote in history.

No nation has struggled more with the Christian biblical legacy in international relations than the United States. This tension is a natural outgrowth of the tensions, rivalries, and debates that have bedeviled American foreign policy since the beginning. The founders who created the United States were products of their Christian faith and the Western Enlightenment. They were rooted in the idealism and rationalism of Jesus and philosophers such as John Locke (himself a Christian) who believed that organic human progress was not only possible but necessary. Thus, the idealism of "human rights" and the pragmatism of national interest have been present in the conduct of United States foreign affairs since the outset. During the founding, a contemporary of that period, the ardent Christian Edmund Burke, developed his ideas based on biblical teachings forming the entire basis of what becomes known as conservatism.

US presidents speak of the freedom agenda, God's gift to humanity, and the nonnegotiable demands of human dignity as the cornerstone of America's role in international affairs. Human dignity is at the very core of the Bible from Genesis 1:27: "So God created man in his own image, in the image of God created he him; male and female created he them." These are the expressed tenets of natural law come full circle to create American foreign policy of the twenty-first century. It is the universal belief that there is a standard to which no man or nation can be the measure but can only aspire. It is the belief that policy must follow from morality and ethics.

It seems clear that the philosophy of the Declaration of Independence was marked by a firm and steadfast belief in natural law, the divine entitlement of liberty, and special providence.

The founding of the United States was based on republican liberty under law, a law grounded in natural law, "written on the heart" of every human being born. Natural law must be a universal law in order for it to be justified in any way. Natural law, then, is critical to understanding America's role in the world, and that heritage comes from the biblical heritage of the Christian faith.

The essence of natural law and natural rights is the belief that there exists a universal order based on ultimate reason or, for Christian scholars, the ultimate reason was given by the Creator. This order dictates universal right and wrong, good and evil. Furthermore, this for Christians is a law that is "written on the heart."

Thinkers like Locke argued that there was a natural law, and thus natural rights that were universal for mankind, emanating ultimately from God. Locke, however, not only sincerely adhered to the Christian faith, but even believed that God's existence was capable of a rational demonstration by proof, as were the central principles of morality. He argued that the natural rights of all human beings are life, liberty, and estate, and that governments, groups, or individuals cannot take these away. His ideas of natural rights, legitimacy based on the consent of the governed, social contract, and the right of rebellion and revolution form the core of the Declaration of Independence and the intellectual core of Anglo-American conservative foreign policy mixed with the Burkean view of Christian tradition and Christian obligation. It is the fundamental belief that freedom is not what is key but rather liberty—liberty under law governed by a natural order—which is overseen by the Creator. It is the belief that all mankind is subject to the divine will, and that those regimes and leaders that deny this are opposing themselves to the very natural order of the universe.

The biblical influence on national behavior is stark beyond comprehension. It has consumed and continues to consume all of Western civilization. No action of a president or prime minister can be taken without reference, whether they like it or not, to the standards of conduct of the Bible and of Jesus's legacy. He is the universal touchstone of conduct.

Thus, the impact of the Bible on international relations is impossible to calculate. As the Christian must accept the Bible as the literal Word of God, that same Christian can use the dynamics of international affairs to discern God's plans past, present, and future.

For God so loved the world, that he gave his only begotten Son, that whosoever believeth in him should not perish, but have everlasting life.

—JOHN 3:16

Bibliography

The Bible, King James Version

Adkins, Lesley, and Roy A. Adkins. *Handbook to Life in Ancient Rome*. New York, NY: Facts on File, Inc., 2004.

Anderson, Clive, and Brian Edwards. *Evidence for the Bible*. Greenforest, AR: Master Books, 2018.

Bancarz, Steven. "A List of Extra-Biblical Sources for the Historical Jesus." Reasons for Jesus, May 17, 2017. https://reasonsforjesus.com/a-list-of-extra -biblical-sources-for-the-historical-jesus/.

Berry, Joanne, and Nigel Pollard. *The Complete Roman Legions*. London: Thames & Hudson, 2012.

Biography.com. "Pontius Pilate Biography." March 27, 2020. https://www.biog-raphy.com/religious-figure/pontius-pilate.

Borg, Marcus J. "Jesus and Politics." Bible Odyssey. Accessed March 2, 2020. https://www.bibleodyssey.org/en/people/related-articles/jesus-and -politics.

Bradford, M. E. "A Teaching for Americans: Roman History and the Republic's First Identity." The Imaginative Conservative. October 19, 2015. https:// theimaginativeconservative.org/2015/10/a-teaching-for-republicans-ro-man-history-and-the-nations-first-identity.html.

Britt, Steven. "Who's Who in the Empire of the Bible." Beyond Today. March 8, 2018. https://www.ucg.org/beyond-today/beyond-today-magazine/ whos-who-in-the-empires-of-the-bible.

Campbell, Charlie H. *Archeological Evidence for the Bible: Exciting Discoveries Verifying Persons, Places, and Events in the Bible*. Scotts Valley, CA: Cre-ateSpace Independent Publishing Company, 2011.

Campbell, Charlie H. *Scrolls and Stones: Compelling Evidence the Bible Can Be Trusted*. California: ABR Apologetics Ministry, 2014.

Bibliography

Captivating History. *Ancient Egypt: A Captivating Guide to Egyptian History, Ancient Pyramids, Temples, Egyptian Mythology, and Pharaohs Such As Tutankhamun and Cleopatra.* Scotts Valley, CA: CreateSpace Independent Publishing Platform, 2018.

Captivating History. *Ancient Greece: A Captivating Guide to Greek History Starting from the Greek Dark Ages to the End of Antiquity.* Scotts Valley, CA: CreateSpace Independent Publishing Platform, 2018.

Captivating History. *Ancient Israel: A Captivating Guide to the Ancient Israelites, Starting from Their Entry Into Canaan Until the Jewish Rebellions Against the Romans.* Scotts Valley, CA: CreateSpace Independent Publishing Platform, 2018.

Captivating History. *Roman History: A Captivating Guide to Ancient Rome, Including the Roman Republic, the Roman Empire, and the Byzantium.* Scotts Valley, CA: CreateSpace Independent Publishing Platform, 2018.

Captivating History. *The Roman Empire: The Roman Empire: A Captivating Guide to the Rise and Fall of the Roman Empire Including Stories of Roman Emperors Such as Augustus Octavian, Trajan, and Claudius.* Scotts Valley, CA: CreateSpace Independent Publishing Platform, 2018.

Casson, Lionel. *Everyday Life in Ancient Rome.* Baltimore, MD: Johns Hopkins University Press, 1998.

Chaline, Eric. Ancient Greece As It Was: Exploring the City of Athens in 415 BC. Guilford, CT: Globe Pequot Press, 2011.

Colucci, Lamont. *Crusading Realism: The Bush Doctrine and American Core Values After 9/11.* Lanham, MD: Rowman & Littlefield, 2008.

Colucci, Lamont. *The National Security Doctrines of the American Presidency: How they Shape Our Present and Future,* a two-volume set in the Praeger Security International series, 2012.

Cornelius Tacitus. *The Annals and History of Tacitus.* London: Forgotten Books, 2012.

Dando-Collins, Stephen. *Legions of Rome: The Definitive History of Every Imperial Roman Legion.* New York, NY: Random House Publisher Services, 2010.

Deffinbaugh, Bob. "The Conversion of Cornelius (Acts 10:36–48)." Bible.org. August13,2004.https://bible.org/seriespage/16-conversion-cornelius-acts-1036-48.

Goldsworthy, Adrian. *Roman Warfare.* New York, NY: Basic Books, 2019.

Goldsworthy, Adrian. *Vindolanda.* London: Head of Zeus, 2018.

Goldsworthy, Adrian. *Pax Romana: War, Peace, and Conquest in the Roman World.* New Haven, CT: Yale University Press, 2016.

Goodman, Martin. *Rome and Jerusalem: The Clash of Ancient Civilizations.* New York, NY: Vintage Books, 2008.

Great Thinkers. "An Introduction to the Work of Augustine." Accessed April 15, 2020. https://thegreatthinkers.org/augustine/introduction/.

Hazony, Yoram. *The Virtue of Nationalism.* New York, NY: Basic Books, 2018.

Hopkins, John. "The Roman Military in the New Testament." Bible.org. June 18, 2010. https://bible.org/article/roman-military-new-testament.

Internet Encyclopedia of Philosophy. "Augustine (354–430 C.E.)." Accessed April 15, 2020. https://www.iep.utm.edu/augustin/.

Internet Encyclopedia of Philosophy. "Thomas Aquinas (1224/6–1274)." Accessed April 15, 2020. https://www.iep.utm.edu/aquinas/.

Jones, Alonzo Trévier. *Empires of the Bible.* Fort Oglethorpe, GA: TEACH Services, Inc., 2004.

Jones, Jonathan. "Cicero and Conservatism." First Things. June 24, 2009. https://www.firstthings.com/blogs/firstthoughts/2009/06/cicero-and -conservatism.

Josephus, Flavius. *The Complete Works of Flavius Josephus: History of the Jewish War against the Romans, The Antiquities of the Jews, Against Apion, Discourse to the Greeks Concerning Hades & Autobiography.* Scotland: T. Nelson Publishers, 1998.

Keller, Werner. *The Bible as History.* New York, NY: Barnes and Noble Books, 1995.

Killen, William Dool. *The Ancient Church: Scholars Choice Decision.* Charleston, SC: Bibliolife, DBA of BibilioBazaar II LLC, 2015.

Kleist, James A. *The Epistles of St. Clement of Rome and St. Ignatius of Antioch.* Mahwah, New Jersey: Paulist Press, 1978.

Laurence, Ray. *The Roman Empire: Rome and Its Environs.* Metro Books, 2008.

Lendering, Jona. "P. Sulpicius Quirinius." Livius.org. April 28, 2020. https://www.livius.org/articles/person/quirinius-p-sulpicius/.

Lendering, Jona. "Pontius Pilate." Livius.org. February 23, 2019. https://www.livius.org/articles/person/pontius-pilate/.

Leston, Dr. Stephen, and Christopher D. Hudson. *The Bible in World History.* Uhrichsville, OH: Barbour Publishing, 2017.

Limbaugh, David. *Jesus Has Risen: Paul and the Early Church.* Washington, DC: Regnery Publishing, 2018.

Maier, Paul L. *Eusebius—The Church History: A New Translation with Commentary.* Grand Rapids, MI: Kregel Publications, 1999.

Nardo, Don. *Life of a Roman Soldier.* San Diego, CA: Lucent Books, 2001.

Perdue, Leo G., Warren Carter, and Coleman A. Baker. *Israel and Empire: A Postcolonial History of Israel and Early Judaism*. London: Bloomsbury, 2015.

Pitre, Brant. *The Case for Jesus: The Biblical and Historical Evidence for Christ*. New York, NY: IMAGE, 2016.

Pliny the Younger. *Complete Letters*. New York, NY: Oxford University Press, 2006.

Podany, Amanda H. *The Brotherhood of Kings: How International Relations Shaped the Ancient Near East*. New York, NY: Oxford University Press, 2010.

Provan, Iain, V. Philips Long, and Tremper Longman III. *A Biblical History of Israel*. Kentucky: self-published, 2003.

River, Charles. *The Roman Province of Judea: The Turbulent History and Legacy of Rome's Rule in Ancient Israel and Judah*. Scotts Valley, CA: CreateSpace Independent Publishing Platform, 2017.

Rozic, Peter. "Church and State: In Defense of Augustine's Allegory of the Two Cities." Reformed Journal. May 1, 2014. https://reformedjournal.com/church-and-state-in-defense-of-augustines-allegory-of-the-two-cities/.

Schwartz, Seth. *Imperialism and Jewish Society: 200 B.C.E. to 640 C.E.* Princeton, NJ: Princeton University Press, 2001.

Shelton, Jo-Ann. *As the Romans Did: A Source Book in Roman Social History*. New York, NY: Oxford University Press, 1998.

Southern, Pat. *The Roman Army: A Social and Institutional History*. Self-published, 2006.

Suetonius, *The Lives of the Caesars, Vol. II: Claudius. Nero. Galba, Otho, Vitellius. Vespasian. Titus, Domitian*. Cambridge, MA: Harvard University Press, 1914.

Suetonius. *The Lives of the Caesars, Vol. I—Julius. Augustus. Tiberius. Gaius. Caligula*. Cambridge, MA: Harvard University Press, 1914.

The Pangea Blog. "Behind Luke's Gospel: The Roman Empire During the Time of Jesus." Accessed March 2, 2020. https://www.patheos.com/blogs/thepangeablog/articles/unpublished-papers/behind-lukes-gospel-the-roman-empire-during-the-time-of-jesus/.

Wallace, Daniel B. "The Problem of Luke 2:2." Bible.org. June 24, 2004. https://bible.org/article/problem-luke-22-ithis-was-first-census-taken-when-quirinius-was-governor-syriai.

Webster, Graham. *The Roman Imperial Army of the First and Second Centuries A.D.*, 3rd ed. Norman, OK: University of Oklahoma Press, 1998.

Willems, Kurt. "The Roman Empire During the Time of Jesus (Background of Luke's Gospel)." Theology Curator. April 8, 2017. https://theologycurator. com/roman-empire-during-time-jesus/.

Woolf, Greg. *Rome: An Empire's Story*. New York, NY: Oxford University Press, 2012.

About the Author

Dr. Lamont Colucci has experience as a diplomat with the U.S. Dept. of State and is a professor of politics at Ripon College. He has authored and contributed to many published books, including *Crusading Realism, The National Security Doctrines of the American Presidency, The Impact of 9/11 on Politics and War,* and *Homeland Security and Intelligence.* He has a doctorate in politics from the University of London, England. He is an occasional columnist for the *Washington Times, National Review, Weekly Standard,* The Hill, U.S. News & World Report, and *Defense News.* He is a bi-monthly columnist for Newsmax. He is also Senior Fellow at the American Foreign Policy Council, Contingent Security, and the Conference of Defence Associations Institute. In 2018, he was appointed to the Task Force on National and Homeland Security.